A Country Store In Your Mailbox®

Gooseberry Patch
600 London Road
P.O. Box 190
Delaware, OH 43015

www.gooseberrypatch.com

1·800·854·6673

Copyright 2009, Gooseberry Patch 978-1-9334948-9-0
Second Printing, January, 2010

Do you have a tried & true recipe...

tip, craft or memory that you'd like to see featured in a **Gooseberry
Patch** cookbook? Visit our website at **www.gooseberrypatch.com**,
register and follow the easy steps to submit your favorite family recipe.
Or send them to us at:

Gooseberry Patch
Attn: Cookbook Dept.
P.O. Box 190
Delaware, OH 43015

Don't forget to include the number of servings your recipe makes,
plus your name, address, phone number and email address.
If we select your recipe, your name will appear right along with
it...and you'll receive a **FREE** copy of the cookbook!

CONTENTS

DEDICATION

This book is dedicated to farmers' markets everywhere...villages, towns, and cities all across the USA!

APPRECIATION

Sending a big farmgirl "Thanks!" to all who shared their best recipes with us!

Summertime Tomato Tart

Linda Belon
Wintersville, OH

*This is so good...a great recipe for your abundance
of tomatoes on the vine!*

4 tomatoes, sliced
9-inch pie crust
8-oz. pkg. shredded mozzarella
   cheese

2 T. fresh basil, chopped
1/4 c. olive oil

Arrange tomato slices in bottom of pie crust. Sprinkle evenly with
cheese and basil; drizzle with oil. Bake at 400 degrees for
30 minutes. Let stand for 5 minutes before slicing. Serves 6.

*No more trying to keep tomato plants upright in the garden!
Plant pint-size cherry tomato plants in hanging baskets filled
with potting soil. They'll grow beautifully...upside-down!*

Golden Zucchini Crescent Pie

*Diane Cohen
The Woodlands, TX*

Delicious served with fresh fruit or a tossed green salad.

8-oz. tube refrigerated crescent
  rolls
2 zucchini, sliced and quartered
1/2 c. onion, chopped
1/4 c. butter, cubed
2 t. fresh parsley, chopped
1/2 t. garlic powder
1/4 t. dried basil

1/4 t. dried oregano
1/2 t. pepper
2 eggs, beaten
8-oz. pkg. shredded mozzarella
  cheese
3/4 c. cooked ham, cubed
1 tomato, thinly sliced

Separate crescent dough into 8 triangles; place in a greased 9" pie
plate with points toward the center. Press onto bottom and up sides of
pie plate to form a crust; press seams together. Bake at 375 degrees
for 5 to 8 minutes, until lightly golden. In a skillet over medium heat,
cook zucchini and onion in butter until tender; stir in parsley and
seasonings. Spoon into crust. Combine remaining ingredients, except
tomato; pour over zucchini mixture. Top with tomato slices. Bake at
375 degrees for 20 to 25 minutes, until a knife inserted near center
comes out clean. Let stand for 5 minutes before cutting. Serves 6.

Don't miss out on the fun! The farmers' market is the very heart
of a community. Every Saturday morning it's a place to find
folks chatting with friends...a place where the joys
of a good, old-fashioned gathering can still be found.

Apple-Cinnamon Pancakes

Cindy Whitney
Bar Mills, ME

A recipe I served my family 12 years ago has become a tradition ever since. We always enjoy picking our own fresh McIntosh apples here in Maine. Half the fun in picking is imagining all the treats you can create. I love pancakes, pies, cookies, apple pan dowdy, baked apples... the list is endless!

1/4 c. powdered buttermilk
   blend
1 c. all-purpose flour
1 T. sugar
1 t. baking powder
1/2 t. baking soda
1/4 t. salt
1 t. cinnamon

1 egg, beaten
1 c. water
2 T. oil
1 McIntosh apple, cored,
   quartered and grated
Garnish: maple syrup, butter,
   whipped cream

Sift together dry ingredients; set aside. Whisk together egg, water and oil; add to dry ingredients. Stir batter until smooth; don't overbeat. Pour batter by 1/4 cupfuls onto a lightly greased hot griddle. Cook until bubbles appear on the surface. Sprinkle with one to 2 teaspoons apple; turn and continue cooking for an additional 2 to 3 minutes, until golden. Serve warm and garnish as desired. Serves 4.

Make pancakes even more yummy. Sprinkle the griddle with
a bit of sugar, then top with an apple slice. Spoon batter over
apple and cook until bubbles form around the edges; flip
with a spatula and cook until golden.

Berry-Picker's Reward Muffins

Nancy Porter
Fort Wayne, IN

This recipe works well with blueberries and strawberries too.

1/2 c. margarine, softened
1-1/4 c. sugar
2 eggs, beaten
8-oz. container sour cream
1 t. vanilla extract
2 c. all-purpose flour

1 t. baking powder
1/2 t. baking soda
1/4 t. salt
1 c. raspberries
3 T. margarine, melted

With an electric mixer on medium-high speed, beat softened margarine for 30 seconds. Add sugar; beat until combined. Blend in eggs, sour cream and vanilla. Use a spoon to stir in dry ingredients until just moistened; fold in berries. Spoon batter into paper-lined or greased muffin cups, filling 2/3 full. Bake at 400 degrees for 18 to 20 minutes, until a toothpick tests clean. Brush tops of hot muffins with melted margarine; sprinkle with topping. Cool in pan for 5 minutes; transfer to a wire rack to finish cooling. Makes 20.

Topping:

2 T. sugar
1/4 t. cinnamon

1/4 t. nutmeg

Combine all ingredients in a small bowl.

*After a morning spent at the local U-Pick berry farm, you'll
have a stash of terrific wooden berry baskets. They're great
for corralling flea-market treasures like vintage buttons
and button cards, spools of ribbon, baubles and trinkets!*

No-Crust Spinach Quiche

Mary Mayall
Dracut, MA

Your family will enjoy this easy dish any time of day.

10-oz. pkg. frozen chopped
   spinach, thawed and drained
Optional: 1/2 c. onion or
   mushrooms, chopped

6 eggs, beaten
1/2 c. milk
1 c. shredded Swiss or Cheddar
   cheese

Spread spinach in a greased 9" pie plate. Sprinkle onion and/or mushrooms over top, if desired. Beat together eggs and milk; stir in cheese. Pour egg mixture evenly over top. Bake at 350 degrees for 25 to 35 minutes, until top is golden and a knife tip inserted into center comes out clean. Cool slightly before cutting. Serves 6.

Tuck some fresh spinach in your basket at the farmers' market. It's oh-so simple to substitute in any recipe that calls for frozen chopped spinach. Simply add 10 ounces of fresh baby spinach and 2 tablespoons water to a saucepan. Cook over medium-low heat for 3 minutes. Stir gently until wilted, then rinse in cold water, drain and squeeze dry.

Farmers' Market Omelet

Vickie

*I love visiting the farmers' market bright & early on Saturday
mornings...a terrific way to begin the day!*

1 t. olive oil
2 T. bacon, diced
2 T. onion, chopped
2 T. zucchini, diced

5 cherry tomatoes, quartered
1/4 t. fresh thyme, minced
3 eggs, beaten
1/4 c. fontina cheese, shredded

Heat oil in a skillet over medium-high heat. Add bacon and onion;
cook and stir until bacon is crisp and onion is tender. Add zucchini,
tomatoes and thyme. Allow to cook until zucchini is soft and juice
from tomatoes has slightly evaporated. Lower heat to medium and stir
in eggs. Stir eggs around skillet with a spatula to cook evenly.
Continue to cook, lifting edges to allow uncooked egg to flow
underneath. When eggs are almost fully cooked, sprinkle cheese over
top and fold over. Serves one.

*For the best selection, plan to be at the market first thing in
the morning. Bring along a roomy shoulder bag or basket too,
so it's easy to tote all your goodies home.*

Smith Family Breakfast Bake

Cherylann Smith
Efland, NC

I created this recipe to duplicate one I tasted and loved.
Now my kids and husband love it too!

12-oz. tube refrigerated biscuits, baked and torn
1 lb. ground pork sausage, browned and drained
8 eggs, beaten
2 c. milk
1 sprig fresh rosemary, chopped

1 t. Italian seasoning
1 t. dried basil
1 t. dried oregano
1 t. dried thyme
salt and pepper to taste
8-oz. pkg. shredded Cheddar cheese

Arrange torn biscuits in a lightly greased 13"x9" baking pan. Top with sausage; set aside. Blend eggs and milk with seasonings. Pour over sausage; sprinkle with cheese. Bake, uncovered, at 350 degrees for 30 minutes, or until golden. Serves 12.

Fill a galvanized minnow bucket with cheery sunflowers...
a centerpiece that captures all the nostalgia of summertime.

Aimee's Sausage Bake

Aimee Warner
Gooseberry Patch

It's the apple that makes this breakfast casserole taste so good.

1 doz. eggs, divided
1-1/2 c. milk, divided
1-1/2 c. saltine crackers,
　crushed
1 c. apple, cored, peeled and
　chopped
1/4 c. onion, chopped
1/2 t. pepper, divided

2 lbs. ground pork sausage
3 T. butter
3 T. all-purpose flour
1 c. cottage cheese
1/2 t. salt
Garnish: fresh parsley, thinly
　sliced apples

Whisk together 2 eggs and 1/2 cup milk. Stir in cracker crumbs, apple, onion and 1/4 teaspoon pepper. Stir in sausage and mix well. Firmly pat mixture into a 6-1/2 cup ring mold, then carefully unmold sausage ring onto a wire rack on a greased baking sheet. Bake at 350 degrees for 50 minutes. Transfer to a platter to keep warm. In a 3-quart saucepan, melt butter. Whisk in flour until smooth. Add remaining milk all at once. Cook and stir over medium heat until bubbly. Continue to cook and stir 2 minutes more. Beat together remaining eggs and pepper, adding cottage cheese and salt. Pour into hot milk mixture. Scramble eggs, stirring frequently, until eggs are cooked through, but still moist. Spoon eggs into center of sausage ring and garnish. Serves 12.

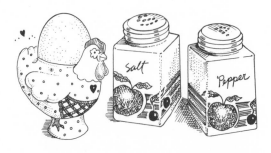

Wake up to colorful pottery on the breakfast table...
so cheery. Search tag sales for whimsical hens on nests
or cream pitcher cows. What treasures!

Grammy's Overnight Pancakes

Regina Ferrigno
Gooseberry Patch

Whenever we visit Grammy, these yummy pancakes are on the breakfast table without fail. Usually they're surrounded by sausage or bacon, scrambled eggs and toast with jam. We can't imagine breakfast any other way!

2 c. long-cooking oats,
   uncooked
2 c. plus 1/4 c. buttermilk,
   divided
1/2 c. all-purpose flour
1/2 c. whole-wheat flour
2 t. sugar
1-1/2 t. baking powder

1-1/2 t. baking soda
1 t. salt
2 eggs, beaten
2 T. butter, melted and cooled
oil for frying
Garnish: butter, warm maple
   syrup

Combine oats and 2 cups buttermilk in a bowl; cover and refrigerate overnight. To prepare pancakes, sift together flours, sugar, baking powder, baking soda and salt. Set aside. In a large bowl, beat together eggs and butter. Stir into oat mixture. Add flour mixture, stirring well. If batter is too thick, stir in 2 to 4 tablespoons remaining buttermilk. Pour batter by heaping tablespoonfuls onto a well-greased hot griddle. Cook until bubbles appear on the surface; turn and continue cooking until golden. Garnish as desired. Makes 2 dozen.

Simple substitutions are at every farmgirl's fingertips.
No buttermilk? Stir one tablespoon vinegar or
lemon juice into one cup milk and let sit 5 minutes.

Fresh Raspberry Butter

Jacinta O'Connell
Kenosha, WI

Substitute blueberries, strawberries, cherries or pineapple.
Scrumptious on toast, waffles or pancakes.

8-oz. pkg. cream cheese,
  softened
1/2 c. butter, softened

1 c. powdered sugar
1 t. vanilla or almond extract
1 c. fresh raspberries, mashed

Combine all ingredients except berries; blend well. Gently fold in raspberries. Cover and refrigerate several hours or overnight. Keep refrigerated for up to one week. Makes 2 cups.

Melon-Berry Bowls

Jill Ball
Highland, UT

I am always looking for healthy, quick and yummy breakfast ideas
for my teenagers. This one has become a favorite!

1 honeydew melon, halved and
  seeded
6-oz. container favorite-flavor
  yogurt

1/2 c. blueberries
1 c. granola cereal

Use a melon baller to scoop melon into balls. Combine melon with remaining ingredients. Spoon into individual bowls to serve. Serves 2 to 4.

Grandma's flowered dessert bowls are just the right size
to fill with homemade berry butter or jam.

Farm-Style Cinnamon Rolls

Cindy Adams
Winona Lake, IN

There's nothing like waking up to the aroma
of baking cinnamon rolls.

16-oz. pkg. frozen bread
   dough, thawed
1/4 c. butter, melted and divided

1/4 c. sugar
1/4 c. brown sugar, packed
1 t. cinnamon

Place dough in a well-oiled bowl and let rise to almost double in size. Roll out dough on a floured surface to a 14-inch by 10-inch rectangle. Brush with 2 tablespoons butter; sprinkle with sugars and cinnamon. Starting on one long side, roll up jelly-roll style. Pinch seam together. Cut roll into 12 slices. Coat the inside of a 9"x9" baking pan with one tablespoon butter. Arrange rolls in baking pan; brush with remaining butter. Cover and let rise in a warm place for 45 minutes to one hour. Uncover and bake at 375 degrees for 20 to 25 minutes, until lightly golden. Makes one dozen.

Grandma knew how to remove stains from a favorite
tablecloth. Combine half a teaspoon of salt with a tablespoon
of water. Wet the stain and lay the tablecloth in the sun.
After an hour, gently rinse the cloth with cold water.

Blueberry Buckle Coffee Cake

Kathy Grashoff
Fort Wayne, IN

Fresh blueberries are a summertime treat to be savored.

2 c. all-purpose flour
3/4 c. sugar
2-1/2 t. baking powder
3/4 t. salt
1/4 c. shortening

3/4 c. milk
2 c. blueberries
1/2 c. powdered sugar
1/4 t. vanilla extract
1/2 to 2 t. hot water

Mix together all ingredients except berries, powdered sugar, vanilla and water. Beat for 30 seconds; carefully fold in berries. Spread batter into a greased 9"x9" baking pan; sprinkle with Crumb Topping. Bake at 375 degrees for 45 to 50 minutes. Combine remaining ingredients in a small bowl; drizzle over warm cake. Makes 9 servings.

Crumb Topping:

1/2 c. sugar
1/3 c. all-purpose flour

1/4 c. butter, softened
1/2 t. cinnamon

Mix all ingredients together until crumbly.

Blueberries, raspberries, mulberries and strawberries are all scrumptious. For a flavorful change, mix & match berries in muffin, coffee cake and quick bread recipes.

Lake House Eggs

Jill Duvendack
Nettle Lake, OH

*We love having our grandchildren with us at our cottage
on the lake. I made this for their first visit, and now
they ask if they're going to have "the eggs."*

10 slices bacon
8-oz. pkg. sliced mushrooms
16 eggs, beaten
1 c. milk
1/2 t. salt
1/4 t. pepper

10-3/4 oz. can nacho cheese
 soup
4 plum tomatoes, chopped
8-oz. pkg. shredded sharp
 Cheddar cheese

In a large skillet over medium-high heat, cook bacon until crisp.
Remove bacon from skillet and crumble, reserving one tablespoon of
drippings in skillet. Cook mushrooms in drippings until tender; set
aside. Blend eggs, milk, salt and pepper; cook over medium heat until
eggs are set, but moist. Fold in remaining ingredients; stir in reserved
bacon. Heat through. Serves 8.

*If you find yourself with extra eggs on hand, it's easy to freeze
them for use later in recipes that will be thoroughly cooked
or baked. Whisk eggs well and pour into a freezer-safe
container. Be sure to label each container with the number
of eggs inside, then freeze. To thaw, place the container
in the refrigerator overnight, and use immediately.*

Berry Cheesecake Muffins

Debi DeVore
Dover, OH

Muffins are even better with a delicious cheesecake filling...yum!

1/3 c. butter, softened	1-1/2 t. baking powder
3/4 c. sugar	1-1/2 t. cinnamon, divided
2 eggs, beaten	1/3 c. milk
1-3/4 c. all-purpose flour,	2 T. brown sugar, packed
divided	1 T. chilled butter

Blend together 1/3 cup butter and sugar; add eggs and beat well.
Combine 1-1/2 cups flour, baking powder and one teaspoon
cinnamon; add to butter mixture alternately with milk. Fill greased or
paper-lined muffin cups half full. Drop Cream Cheese Filling by
tablespoonfuls into centers of muffins. Combine remaining flour,
brown sugar and remaining cinnamon in a small bowl. Cut in
remaining butter until crumbly and sprinkle over batter. Bake at
375 degrees for 25 to 30 minutes, or until a toothpick comes out
clean. Cool for 5 minutes before removing to a wire rack. Serve warm.
Makes 1-1/2 dozen.

Cream Cheese Filling:

2 3-oz. pkgs. cream cheese,	1 egg, beaten
softened	3/4 c. blueberries
1/3 c. sugar	3/4 c. raspberries

In a small bowl, beat cream cheese, sugar and egg until smooth;
fold in berries.

When spring fever comes
along, delight a friend
with a posy tucked
into a vintage bottle.

Crab, Corn & Pepper Frittata

Stacie Avner
Delaware, OH

This is an adaptation of one of my mom's recipes.
In the summertime, I like to use fresh corn.

6 eggs, beaten
1/4 c. milk
1/3 c. mayonnaise
1 c. imitation crabmeat
2 T. green onion, chopped

2 T. red pepper, chopped
1/3 c. corn
salt and pepper to taste
1 c. shredded Monterey Jack
   cheese

Whisk together all ingredients except cheese. Pour into a greased 10" pie plate. Bake at 350 degrees for 15 to 20 minutes. Sprinkle with cheese and bake for an additional 5 minutes, or until cheese is melted. Serves 4 to 6.

Recycle an old wheelbarrow into a movable garden filled
with herbs, flowers, lettuce or carrots...how clever!

Scrambled Eggs & Lox

Jackie Smulski
Lyons, IL

These eggs are sure to please everyone...excellent with toasted English muffins or bagels.

6 eggs, beaten
1 T. fresh dill, minced
1 T. fresh chives, minced
1 T. green onion, minced

pepper to taste
2 T. butter
4-oz. pkg. smoked salmon, diced

Whisk together eggs, herbs, onion and pepper. Melt butter in a large skillet over medium heat. Add egg mixture and stir gently with a fork or spatula until eggs begin to set. Stir in salmon and continue cooking eggs to desired doneness. Serves 6.

If it's your first visit to the farmers' market, have fun!
Chat with the farmers, see what fresh veggies, fruits
and flowers are available, then get shopping!

Cinnamon Chip Crescents

Lisa Hays
Crocker, MO

Adding cinnamon chips makes these so yummy!

2 8-oz. tubes refrigerated
   crescent rolls
2 T. butter, melted

10-oz. pkg. cinnamon baking
   chips, divided
1-1/2 t. shortening

Separate crescent dough into 16 triangles; brush with butter. Divide one cup cinnamon chips evenly over triangles and gently press into dough. Roll each triangle from shortest side to the opposite point. Arrange point-side down on an ungreased baking sheet and curve each into a crescent shape. Bake at 375 degrees for 8 to 10 minutes, until golden; set aside. Combine remaining chips and shortening in a microwave-safe dish. Heat on high setting for one minute; stir until chips are melted and mixture is smooth. Drizzle over crescent rolls. Serve warm. Makes 16.

No matter what the recipe, try swapping out
chocolate chips to create a brand-new treat.
Butterscotch, cinnamon, vanilla, cherry and mint chips
will make a yummy cookie, muffin or sweet treat.

Peanut Butter Muffins

Amy Tucker
British Columbia, Canada

My mother encouraged us kids to eat a healthy breakfast in the morning, but sometimes this was challenging because we liked to sleep in. Breakfast was often on the go, so she created this recipe just for us. Now I make them for my children.

1 c. whole-wheat flour
1 c. long-cooking oats,
   uncooked
1 T. baking soda
1/2 t. salt
1/4 c. creamy peanut butter

1/3 c. applesauce
Optional: 1 c. chopped nuts,
   1 c. raisins
1-1/2 c. milk
1/4 c. honey, maple syrup or
   molasses

Whisk together flour, oats, baking soda and salt. Add peanut butter and applesauce; beat with an electric mixer on low speed until smooth. Stir in nuts and raisins, if using. Stir in milk and honey, syrup or molasses. Spoon batter into paper-lined or greased muffin cups, filling 2/3 full. Bake at 350 degrees for 12 to 15 minutes, until a toothpick tests clean. Cool in pan 5 minutes; transfer to a wire rack to finish cooling. Makes 1-1/2 dozen.

Bring along a thermos of milk to the market...sometimes those home-baked goodies just can't wait to be enjoyed!

Bensons' Ultimate Pancakes

Triann Benson
Plano, TX

*My husband and I enjoy entertaining and sometimes the best
get-together is a Saturday morning brunch. We came up with this recipe
by combining the best of several different recipes. The whipped egg
whites are the secret ingredient!*

3 T. butter, melted
1 T. vanilla extract
1-1/2 c. all-purpose flour
1 T. baking powder
1 t. salt
1 T. sugar

1-1/4 c. milk
1 egg yolk, beaten
2 egg whites
1-1/2 to 2 c. blueberries
Garnish: butter, maple syrup,
    whipped cream, blueberries

Combine all ingredients except egg whites, blueberries and garnish in
a large bowl. With an electric mixer on high speed, beat egg whites
until stiff. Gently fold into batter. Pour batter by 1/3 cupfuls onto a
greased hot griddle. Spoon several blueberries on top of just-poured
batter. Cook until bubbles appear on the surface; turn and continue
cooking for an additional 2 to 3 minutes, until golden. Garnish as
desired. Makes about one dozen.

*Top pancakes with something other than syrup...spoonfuls of
fruity jams or homemade preserves, fresh berries and a dusting
of powdered sugar, or a drizzle of honey are all scrumptious.*

Lemon Curd Tartlets

Margaret Welder
Madrid, IA

This filling is delicious as a topping for
blueberry pancakes or muffins too.

1/2 c. sugar
1/4 c. butter
3 T. lemon juice
1 egg, beaten
1 t. lemon zest

1/4 c. whipping cream
2 T. powdered sugar
2 2.1-oz. pkgs. frozen
   pre-baked phyllo tart shells

Combine sugar, butter and lemon juice in the top of a double boiler over hot water. Cook and stir over medium heat until butter melts and sugar is dissolved. Reduce heat to low and continue cooking for 2 minutes. Place egg in a small bowl; whisk continually while slowly adding 1/4 cup sugar mixture. Pour mixture into the top of double boiler; add zest. Cook over medium heat, stirring constantly, for about 15 minutes, until mixture thickens and coats the back of a spoon. Remove mixture to a bowl; cover with plastic wrap and cool. With an electric mixer on high speed, beat whipping cream with powdered sugar until soft peaks form. Fold into chilled lemon curd; cover and refrigerate. When ready to serve, spoon one tablespoon of curd into each tart shell. Makes 32.

After enjoying an orange or grapefruit for breakfast, don't toss the hollowed-out fruit halves. Filled with potting soil, seeds and a nice drink of water, these clever little starter pots can be planted directly in your garden!

Breakfast Apple Pie

Lori Ritchey
Denver, PA

Who says pie isn't for breakfast? Share this yummy,
easy-to-tote breakfast treat with your neighbors.

1 egg, beaten
1/4 c. oil
1 c. milk
1-1/2 c. biscuit baking mix
1/2 c. plus 2 T. sugar, divided
Optional: 1/2 c. chopped
    walnuts or pecans

2 apples, cored and cut into
    wedges
1/2 t. cinnamon
1/4 t. nutmeg
2 T. butter, diced
Garnish: whipped cream or
    vanilla ice cream

Beat together egg, oil and milk; add biscuit mix, 1/2 cup sugar and
nuts, if using. Beat well. Pour into a greased 9" pie plate. Arrange
apple wedges over batter; sprinkle with remaining sugar, cinnamon
and nutmeg. Dot with butter. Bake at 375 degrees for 30 minutes, or
until apples are tender. Serve warm with whipped cream or vanilla ice
cream. Serves 4 to 6.

For the best pie apples, you can always count
on Jonathan, Winesap, Braeburn, Fuji,
Rome Beauty, Granny Smith and Pippin apples.

Herbed Mushroom Omelets

Jo Ann

*Use any favorites from your herb garden...
rosemary and chives are really good too.*

4 to 6 eggs, beaten
1 T. fresh parsley, chopped
1 t. fresh oregano, chopped
1/2 t. fresh thyme, chopped

salt and pepper to taste
2 t. butter, divided
1-1/2 c. sliced mushrooms

Whisk together eggs and seasonings; set aside. Melt one teaspoon butter in a skillet over medium heat. Add mushrooms and sauté until tender; remove from skillet and set aside. Melt 1/2 teaspoon butter in skillet over low heat; pour in half the egg mixture. Stir eggs around in skillet with a spatula to cook evenly. Lift edges to allow uncooked egg to flow underneath. When almost cooked, spoon on half the mushrooms and fold over. Repeat with remaining egg mixture. Serves 2.

*Herbs are easy to grow...even indoors on a sunny windowsill.
Fragrant and tasty, try adding snips of rosemary, oregano,
savory, parsley, sage, thyme or chives for flavoring
sauces and salads.*

Grandma McKindley's Waffles

Nicole Millard
Mendon, MI

My great-grandmother lived to be almost 100 years old. She was a simple and genuinely kind person, as well as a great cook. She always had time for her children, grandchildren and great-grandchildren. Whenever we came to visit, she would stop what she was doing and teach us all kinds of songs or sayings. She made her home such a nice place to visit.

2 c. all-purpose flour	2 eggs, separated
1 T. baking powder	1-1/2 c. milk
1/4 t. salt	3 T. butter, melted

Sift together flour, baking powder and salt; set aside. With an electric mixer on high speed, beat egg whites until stiff; set aside. Stir egg yolks, milk and melted butter together; add to dry ingredients, stirring just until moistened. Fold in egg whites. Ladle batter by 1/2 cupfuls onto a lightly greased preheated waffle iron; bake according to manufacturer's directions. Makes 8 to 10 waffles.

There's just something wonderful about finding the "perfect"
auction or sale. Then there's the fun of coming home with
an armload of canning jars, baskets and watering cans to
hold just-cut flowers. Look for vintage fabrics too...
they make terrific jar toppers for jams & jellies.

Apple Pie Oatmeal

Nichole Stalnaker
Beverly, MA

A slow-cooker breakfast the whole family will enjoy.

2-1/2 c. milk
1 c. steel-cut oats, uncooked
2 T. brown sugar, packed
2 T. honey
1 T. butter, melted
1 T. apple pie spice

1 T. ground flaxseed
1 green apple, cored and
   chopped
1/2 c. raisins
1/2 c. chopped walnuts
1/8 t. salt

Place all ingredients into a slow cooker sprayed with non-stick vegetable spray. Stir well to combine. Cover and cook on low setting for 6 to 8 hours. Serves 4.

Put the slow cooker to work for any meal. It does all
the cooking so there's plenty of time to stitch up
a ruffly garden apron!

Carol's Famous Pancakes

Carol Odachowski
Wakefield, MA

*These pancakes are so delicious, you will want to double
the recipe to make plenty of extras for everyone!*

1 egg, beaten
2/3 c. milk
1/4 c. oil
1 c. all-purpose flour

2 t. baking powder
1/4 t. baking soda
1/2 c. powdered sugar

Combine egg, milk and oil in a bowl; sift together remaining
ingredients and stir into egg mixture until well blended. Pour by
1/4 cupfuls onto a lightly greased hot griddle. Cook until bubbles
appear on the surface; turn and continue cooking for an additional
2 to 3 minutes. Serves 4.

*Dress up a plain canvas shopping tote for trips to the
farmers' market, tag or junk sale...just stitch on
rows and rows of colorful rick rack.*

Fiesta Breakfast Strata

Yvette Nelson
British Columbia, Canada

This is a recipe I created because I love Mexican food. Homemade salsa is easier than you'd think, and every time I make this, I'm asked to share the recipe.

1 lb. ground beef
8-oz. can tomato sauce
2 t. chili powder
1/2 t. garlic powder
salt and pepper to taste
5 10-inch flour tortillas
16-oz. can refried beans, divided

8-oz. pkg. shredded sharp Cheddar cheese, divided
1 red pepper, diced
2 tomatoes, diced
5 green onions, chopped
salt and pepper to taste
Garnish: salsa, sour cream

Brown ground beef in a skillet; drain. Add tomato sauce and seasonings. Simmer until mixture thickens; set aside. Line the bottom of a 9" springform pan with aluminum foil. Place a tortilla in the bottom of the pan. Spread half the refried beans on tortilla and top with half the ground beef mixture. Top with 1/3 of the cheese. Layer a second tortilla over cheese; sprinkle with half each red pepper, tomatoes and onions. Add a third tortilla and spread with remaining refried beans, beef mixture and 1/3 cheese. Layer on a fourth tortilla and top with remaining red pepper and tomatoes. Add last tortilla and cover with remaining cheese and onions. Bake, uncovered, at 350 degrees one hour, or until heated through. Garnish as desired. Serves 6 to 8.

Salsa:

1 orange, red or yellow pepper, diced
1 jalapeño pepper, diced
1/2 red onion, diced

1 tomato, diced
1/2 c. fresh cilantro, chopped
1 T. lemon juice
salt and pepper to taste

Combine all ingredients; refrigerate for one hour.

Make-Ahead French Toast

Carla Turner
Salem, OR

*This wonderful make-ahead dish is perfect for Sunday brunches.
With the prep time being the day before, I'm free to visit
with friends & family.*

5 T. margarine
2 baking apples, cored, peeled
   and sliced
1 c. brown sugar, packed
2 T. dark corn syrup
1 t. cinnamon

8 1-inch thick slices French
   bread
3 eggs, beaten
1 c. milk
1 t. vanilla extract

Melt margarine in a heavy skillet over medium heat. Reduce heat to
medium-low; add apples and cook, stirring occasionally, until tender.
Stir in brown sugar, corn syrup and cinnamon. Cook and stir until
brown sugar dissolves. Pour apple mixture into two lightly greased
9" pie plates or one, 13"x9" baking pan. Arrange bread slices in one
layer on top of apple mixture; set aside. In a medium bowl, whisk
together remaining ingredients; pour over bread slices. Cover with
plastic wrap and refrigerate overnight. Remove plastic wrap and bake
at 375 degrees for 30 to 35 minutes, or until firm and golden. Cool
5 minutes in pan, then invert onto a serving platter. Serves 12 to 15.

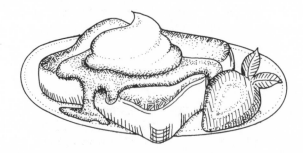

*A spoonful of this lemony spread is tasty on French toast,
pancakes or waffles. Blend a 6-ounce carton of lemon
custard-style yogurt with a 3-ounce package of softened
cream cheese and one tablespoon of honey.*

Quick & Easy Summer Salsa

Chris Nelson
New Berlin, WI

There is absolutely nothing like garden-fresh salsa. If you can't wait for it to chill, no problem...it's terrific enjoyed right away!

10 roma tomatoes, chopped
1 c. fresh cilantro, chopped
1/2 c. red onion, chopped
1 T. vinegar

1/2 c. olive oil
juice of 2 key limes
tortilla chips

Combine all ingredients except chips in a bowl; stir to blend. Refrigerate until chilled. Serve with tortilla chips. Makes 2-1/2 to 3 cups.

Almost any fresh veggie can be added to a favorite salsa recipe. Try stirring in chopped peppers, green onions, minced garlic and sweet corn.

Lynda's Spinach-Feta Dip

Lynda McCormick
Burkburnett, TX

This is a favorite dip enjoyed with bread cubes or crackers.
Try garnishing with some farm-fresh chopped tomatoes too.

8-oz. container Greek yogurt
3/4 c. crumbled feta cheese
1/4 c. cream cheese, softened
1/4 c. sour cream
1 clove garlic, pressed
1-1/2 c. baby spinach, finely
   chopped

1 T. fresh dill, minced, or
   1 t. dill weed
1/8 t. pepper
Optional: additional minced
   fresh dill
pita or bagel chips

Combine yogurt, cheeses, sour cream and garlic in a food processor.
Process until smooth, scraping sides once. Spoon yogurt mixture into
a bowl; stir in spinach, dill and pepper. Cover and refrigerate for
several hours, until chilled. Let stand for 10 minutes at room
temperature before serving. If desired, garnish with additional dill;
serve with chips. Makes 2 cups.

Until they're ready for your best recipe, tuck sprigs of fresh
herbs into water-filled Mason jars or votive holders for a few
days. Not only will they stay fresh longer, they'll look so lovely.

Rocky Mountain Cereal Bars

Karen Ensign
Providence, UT

*Our whole family loves these bars, whether they're for a snack,
dessert or even breakfast.*

2/3 c. sugar
2/3 c. corn syrup
1 c. creamy peanut butter
6 c. doughnut-shaped
   multi-grain oat cereal

3/4 to 1 c. sweetened dried
   cranberries

Combine sugar, corn syrup and peanut butter in a saucepan over low
heat. Stirring constantly, heat through until peanut butter is melted.
Remove from heat. Add cereal and cranberries; mix well. Spread
cereal mixture evenly into a lightly greased 13"x9" baking pan. Cool
completely; cut into bars. Makes about 2-1/2 dozen.

When heading out to the farmers' market, be prepared for all
kinds of weather...from early-morning frost to the heat
of summer sunshine. It's a good idea to toss an umbrella,
sunglasses and even a light jacket in the car before leaving.

Peggy's Granola

Beth Smith
Manchester, MI

When a dear friend put this granola in a gift basket,
my husband and I couldn't stop eating it!

4 c. quick-cooking oats,
  uncooked
2 c. crispy rice cereal
2 c. sliced almonds
2 T. cinnamon

2 c. brown sugar, packed
2/3 c. butter
1/2 c. honey
2 c. raisins or chopped dried
  fruit

Toss oats, cereal, almonds and cinnamon together in a large bowl; set aside. Combine brown sugar, butter and honey in a heavy saucepan over medium-high heat. Boil, stirring occasionally, until butter is melted and brown sugar is dissolved. Pour over oat mixture; stir to coat. Spread evenly on an aluminum foil-lined baking sheet. Bake at 350 degrees for 10 minutes; stir well. Bake for an additional 10 minutes. Remove from oven and cool 5 minutes; transfer to a large bowl. Stir in raisins or fruit and cool completely. Store in airtight containers. Makes 14 cups.

Easy-to-tote snacks like granola are a perfect take-along
while visiting the farmers' market, barn sale or auction.

Minty Orange Iced Tea

Barb Stout
Gooseberry Patch

*Sometimes I find ginger mint or pineapple mint at the
farmers' market and always pick up a bunch.
It's fun to try a new herb in this tea recipe.*

6 c. water
8 teabags
1/4 c. fresh mint, chopped
3 T. sugar

2 c. orange juice
juice of 2 lemons
ice

Bring water to a boil in a saucepan. Remove from heat and add
teabags, mint and sugar; steep for 20 minutes. Discard teabags; strain
out mint. Chill for at least 2 hours. Pour into a large pitcher; add
juices. Serve in tall glasses over ice. Makes 6 to 8 servings.

*Mint is an easy herb to grow and nice in so many recipes.
Planted in a garden though, it tends to spread quickly. To keep
mint only where you want it, it's best to tuck plants into
containers. Keep a variety by the kitchen door...
peppermint, spearmint and applemint.*

Summertime Citrus Tea

Susan Wilson
Johnson City, TN

Try herbal teabags if you like...they'll be just as terrific.

4 c. water
6 teabags
1-1/2 c. sugar
6-oz. can frozen orange juice
    concentrate, thawed

6-oz. can frozen lemonade
    concentrate, thawed
10 c. cold water
ice

Bring water to a boil in a saucepan. Remove from heat and add teabags; steep overnight. Discard teabags. Pour into a large pitcher; add remaining ingredients. Serve in tall glasses over ice. Makes 6 servings.

Southern Honey Ice

Staci Meyers
Montezuma, GA

A great way to complement your favorite beverage...
especially a fruity glass of sweet tea.

2 c. hot water
1/2 c. honey

2 T. lemon juice

Combine all ingredients and pour into an ice cube tray; freeze. Place ice cubes in tall glasses; top with favorite beverage. Makes about one dozen.

Bring small bills along with
some coins for farmers' market
shopping...it makes it so
much easier for the vendors
to give you change.

Heavenly Cheesecake Dip

Barbara Bower
Orrville, OH

Sometimes I even fold in blueberries or strawberries. Yum!

2 1-oz. pkgs. instant sugar-free
  cheesecake pudding mix
24-oz. container plain yogurt

16-oz. container frozen whipped
  topping, thawed
favorite fresh fruit, sliced

Combine dry pudding mixes and yogurt in a bowl; stir until well
blended. Fold in whipped topping; cover and chill. Serve with fresh
fruit for dipping. Makes about 5 cups.

*To keep just-cut fruit slices looking fresh, dip them
into lemon-lime soda before serving.*

Cinnamon-Sugar Crisp Strips

Melissa Fraser
Valencia, CA

When my mother taught me to make this recipe, we used wonton wrappers. I modified it slightly and now use flour tortillas, but both taste great. In fact, once you taste these you'll have trouble walking away from more! Try dipping them in warm cinnamon-apple pie filling...yummy!

1 T. cinnamon
1 c. sugar
oil for deep frying

8 10-inch flour tortillas, cut into 1-inch strips

Combine cinnamon and sugar together in a bowl; set aside. Heat 2 inches of oil in a heavy skillet over medium-high heat. Add 5 to 7 tortilla strips at a time; cook for 20 to 40 seconds on each side until crisp. Drain on a paper towel-lined plate for 5 minutes, then sprinkle with cinnamon-sugar mixture. Place strips and remaining cinnamon-sugar mixture into a paper bag. Gently toss to coat well. Remove from bag and arrange on a serving plate. Makes 6 to 8 servings.

When apples are in season, bring home a bushel and make apple pie filling...for your freezer! Prepare a favorite recipe, then let the pie filling cool for 30 minutes. Spoon it into freezer containers, leaving 1/2-inch headspace. Let cool about an hour, seal containers and freeze for up to one year.

Veggie Mini Pizzas

Elisha Wiggins
Suwanee, GA

*The taste of juicy summertime tomatoes and fresh spinach
is unbeatable on these yummy mini pizzas.*

6 pita rounds
1-1/2 c. pizza or pasta sauce
1 c. baby spinach
2 plum tomatoes, sliced

8-oz. pkg. shredded mozzarella
  cheese
1 T. olive oil

Place pita rounds on an ungreased baking sheet. Spread each with
1/4 cup sauce; top with spinach, tomato and cheese. Drizzle each pita
with 1/2 teaspoon oil. Bake at 350 degrees for 15 to 20 minutes, or
until cheese is bubbly. Makes 6 servings.

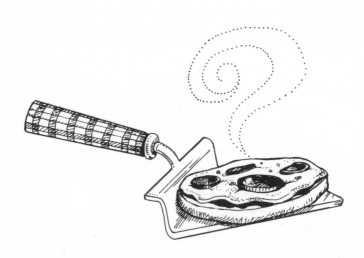

*Gardens turn up the best pizza toppers...
try something new like chopped spinach,
green onions, chives, cilantro, asparagus,
sliced roma tomatoes or shredded carrots.*

Stuffed Cherry Tomatoes

Betty Reeves
Cardington, OH

These little appetizers are a real hit at family picnics, especially with homegrown cherry tomatoes just ripened and picked off the vine. They are so easy to make and simply delicious.

1 lb. bacon, crisply cooked and
   crumbled
24 cherry tomatoes
1/2 c. mayonnaise

1/2 c. green onion, finely
   chopped
2 T. fresh parsley, chopped
salt and pepper to taste

Set aside prepared bacon on paper towels to drain. Cut a thin slice off the top of each tomato; discard slices. Use a small spoon to hollow out tomatoes; discard pulp. Combine remaining ingredients in a bowl; blend well. Spoon mixture into hollowed-out tomatoes. Refrigerate until chilled. Makes 2 dozen.

It's easy to dry fresh herbs…just bunch them together with kitchen twine and hang upside-down. Once they're dry, you can have the flavor of garden-fresh herbs no matter what the season.

43

Tropical Smoothies

Melissa Bordenkircher
Gooseberry Patch

A chilled, fruity smoothie really hits the spot on a summer's day.

1 c. mango, peeled, pitted and
   cubed
3/4 c. banana, sliced
2/3 c. milk

1 t. honey
1/4 t. vanilla extract
Optional: 1 T. powdered milk

Arrange mango in a single layer on a baking sheet; freeze for one hour. Place frozen mango and remaining ingredients in a blender. Process until smooth. Pour into glasses to serve. Serves 2.

Berry-Citrus Smoothies

Cheri Maxwell
Gulf Breeze, FL

A super-tasty, 3-ingredient recipe that's ready in a snap.

1 pt. strawberries, hulled and
   sliced
1 c. buttermilk or plain yogurt

1 c. frozen lemon or orange
   sorbet

Combine all ingredients in a blender; process until smooth. Pour into glasses to serve. Makes 4 servings.

*I have never had so many good ideas day after day
as when I worked in the garden.*

-John Erskine

Celebration Fruit Salsa

Lavonda Wingfield
Boaz, AL

While planning our youngest son's wedding reception, I was looking for just the right recipes. My aunt, who is a terrific cook, shared this one with me. It was a hit from the get-go. I don't know how many times I shared the recipe while I was on the dance floor...everyone just kept asking for it!

1 c. strawberries, hulled and chopped
1 orange, peeled and finely chopped
2 kiwi, peeled and finely chopped
1/2 fresh pineapple, peeled and finely chopped, or 8-oz. can crushed pineapple, drained
1/4 c. green onion, thinly sliced

1/4 c. green or yellow pepper, finely chopped
1 T. lime or lemon juice
1 jalapeño pepper, seeded and chopped
Garnish: fresh parsley, whole strawberries or cantaloupe slices
tortilla chips

Combine all ingredients except garnish and tortilla chips in a bowl; stir well. Refrigerate until chilled. Garnish as desired. Serve with tortilla chips. Makes 3 cups.

Whip up a veggie stir-fry in a flash. Simply combine 2 tablespoons of cornstarch, 2 tablespoons of sugar and 1/2 teaspoon ground ginger. Blend in one cup orange juice and 1/4 cup soy sauce. Toss any of your favorite veggies in a skillet with a bit of oil and cook for about 4 to 5 minutes. Add the orange juice mixture; cook and stir until thickened.

Quilters' Squares

Dolores Brock
Wellton, AZ

My friend Helen shared this recipe with me...she would always prepare it for our quilters' meetings. Now, whenever I make it, I think of her and the sweet little hat she always wore.

1 lb. ground beef
1 lb. ground pork sausage
1 onion, chopped
16-oz. pkg. pasteurized process
   cheese spread, cubed

1 T. Worcestershire sauce
1/2 t. garlic salt
1/2 t. dried oregano
2 T. fresh parsley, minced
1 loaf sliced party rye

Brown beef, pork and onion in a skillet over medium heat; drain. Add remaining ingredients except rye slices. Cook and stir until cheese is melted. Arrange rye slices on an ungreased baking sheet. Spread each with one tablespoon beef mixture. Bake at 450 degrees for 8 minutes, or until bubbly. Makes 3 dozen.

Once summertime herbs have dried, store them in jars with biscuit-topper lids...how clever! Search flea markets for biscuit cutters, then purchase new jars whose lids will fit inside the cutters. Secure new lids inside the cutters with metal adhesive and let dry.

California Spinach Snackers

Kimberly Hancock
Murrieta, CA

*These are so tasty, sometimes I make two batches
because they go so fast!*

1 T. butter
1/2 c. onion, finely chopped
10-oz. pkg. frozen chopped
   spinach, thawed
3/4 c. mayonnaise
8-oz. pkg. shredded mozzarella
   cheese

1-1/2 t. nutmeg
16.3-oz. tube refrigerated
   buttermilk biscuits
salt and pepper to taste

Melt butter in a saucepan over medium heat. Add onion and cook
until tender; drain. In a bowl, combine onion, spinach, mayonnaise,
cheese and nutmeg; set aside. Unroll biscuit dough; divide each in half
horizontally. Press biscuit halves into lightly greased mini muffin
cups. Shape each into small cups that extend slightly beyond the rim.
Fill with spinach mixture. Bake at 375 degrees for 12 minutes, or
until biscuits are lightly golden. Serve warm or at room temperature.
Makes 16.

*Add a burst of flavor to a glass of water...
toss in fresh berries, melon or apple slices.*

Honey-Glazed Snack Mix

Cindy Elliott
Modesto, IL

This recipe is from my friend, Mary Beth Mitchell. Our sons, who are now 15 years old, went to preschool together. I like the taste of this best when I use fresh honey from the farmers' market or orchard.

5 c. corn & rice cereal
3 c. mini pretzel twists
2 c. pecan halves

1/2 c. honey
1/2 c. margarine, melted

Combine cereal, pretzels and pecans in a large bowl; set aside. Blend together honey and margarine. Pour over cereal mixture; toss to coat. Spread on ungreased baking sheets. Bake at 300 degrees for 10 minutes. Stir and continue to bake an additional 10 to 15 minutes. Pour onto wax paper and cool completely. Store in airtight containers. Makes about 10 cups.

Honey has a variety of flavors...it might have a hint of berries, clover or wildflowers. Ask the vendors which is their favorite and why...they may even have a few recipes to share.

Old-Fashioned Movie Popcorn

Laura Slater
Bakersfield, CA

So much better tasting than microwave popcorn. Try sprinkling with grated Parmesan cheese, seasoning salt or sugar.

1/4 c. oil
1/4 c. unpopped popcorn

2 T. butter, melted
1 t. salt

Heat oil in a heavy saucepan over medium-high heat. Add popcorn and cover. Once popping begins, gently shake the pan by moving it back and forth over the burner. Keep the lid slightly ajar to let steam escape. Once popping slows to several seconds between pops, remove pan from heat and pour popcorn into a large bowl. Drizzle with butter; add salt to taste. Makes about 8 cups.

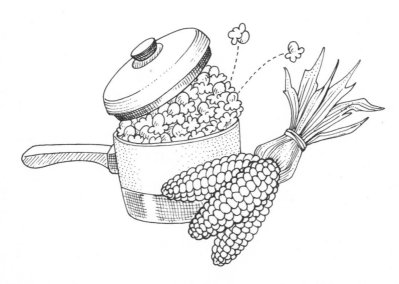

In the Midwest, you can find farmers who sell homegrown popcorn at the market! To remove the kernels, hold an ear firmly in both hands and twist until the kernels drop off. Pop kernels the old-fashioned way, on the stove, or in a microwave popcorn popper.

Spring Tonic

Charlotte Page
Jay, ME

A sweet-tart drink that's oh-so refreshing
when spring comes around.

2 lbs. rhubarb, chopped
4 c. water

3/4 to 1 c. sugar
ice

Combine rhubarb and water in a saucepan; simmer over medium-low heat until rhubarb is soft. Strain and discard rhubarb, reserving liquid. Pour into a large pitcher; add sugar to taste. Chill until ready to serve. Serve in tall glasses over ice. Makes 3 to 4 quarts.

Oh-So-Fruity Lemonade

Jamie Johnson
Gooseberry Patch

When it's time to cool off on a summer day, a tall glass
of this frosty lemonade will do the trick!

12-oz. can frozen lemonade
  concentrate, thawed
2 c. cold water
1-1/2 c. mango juice
1/2 c. red or green grapes,
  halved
1/2 c. pineapple, chopped

1/2 c. mango, peeled, pitted and
  chopped
1/2 c. strawberries, hulled and
  chopped
1/2 c. raspberries
ice

Combine lemonade concentrate, water and juice in a large pitcher. Stir in fruit. Serve immediately over ice, or cover and chill up to one hour. Makes 2 quarts.

Snap up roomy gallon-size Mason jars when you spot them...
just right for holding lots of iced tea or lemonade.

Sweet & Tangy Fruit Dip

Jill Ball
Highland, UT

As a mother, I'm always looking for easy, healthy snack ideas,
so I created this recipe. My children love it, and so do I...
it's different, yummy and healthy for them.

1 c. cottage cheese
3 T. plain yogurt
2 t. honey
1 T. orange juice

2-1/2 T. orange marmalade
2 T. sweetened flaked coconut
favorite fresh fruit, sliced

Place all ingredients except coconut and fruit in a food processor. Process until smooth and creamy. Stir in coconut. Refrigerate until chilled. Serve with a variety of fresh fruit. Makes 10 servings.

Keep fruit dip chilled in a vintage pie plate
filled with crushed ice. Nestle a bowl into the
ice to keep the dip chilled...country style!

Country Herb Spread

Cindy Brown
Farmington Hills, MI

For variety, omit chives and dill; add one teaspoon fresh oregano and 1/2 teaspoon each fresh thyme, basil and marjoram.

8-oz. pkg. cream cheese,
   softened
1 T. mayonnaise
1 t. Dijon mustard

1 T. fresh chives, chopped
1 T. fresh dill, chopped
1 clove garlic, pressed
crackers

Combine all ingredients except crackers; stir until well blended. Serve with crackers. Makes 1-1/2 cups.

Fiesta Guacamole

Marian Smith
Gooseberry Patch

This was a tasty addition to our office Fiesta Party!

4 avocados, peeled, pitted,
   cubed and mashed
2 tomatoes, diced
1/2 onion, diced

1 bunch fresh cilantro, chopped
1 jalapeño pepper, chopped
1 T. garlic, minced
juice of 2 limes

Blend together avocados and tomatoes. Stir in onion, cilantro, jalapeño and garlic. Add lime juice; mix well. Cover and refrigerate for 45 minutes before serving. Makes 10 servings.

Spooned over avocado halves, Santa Fe-style dressing is so yummy! Combine 2 tablespoons mayonnaise with 1/4 teaspoon garlic powder, 1/8 teaspoon red pepper flakes and 1/2 teaspoon cumin. Stir in some finely chopped fresh cilantro and chill 30 minutes.

Savory Stuffed Mushrooms

Francie Stutzman
Dalton, OH

Oh, are these so good! Depending on the size
of the mushrooms, this makes 40 to 50.

1 lb. whole mushrooms
1/4 c. oil, divided
1/4 c. onion, minced
1 clove garlic, minced
1/4 lb. cooked ham, ground
1/2 c. dry bread crumbs

2 T. grated Parmesan cheese
1 egg, beaten
1 T. fresh parsley, chopped
1 t. fresh oregano, chopped
1/2 t. salt
1/8 t. pepper

Remove mushroom stems and chop enough to equal 1/2 cup. Set aside. Heat 2 tablespoons oil in a skillet over medium heat; add mushroom caps and stir to coat with oil. Remove and set aside on paper towels to drain. Add chopped stems to skillet with onion and garlic. Cook over medium-high heat for 10 minutes. Remove skillet from heat and add remaining ingredients. Spoon mixture into mushroom caps. Arrange on an ungreased baking sheet; drizzle tops with remaining oil. Bake at 325 degrees for 30 minutes. Makes 40 to 50 stuffed mushrooms.

Roasted garlic is delicious spread over slices of French bread.
Simply peel away the skin from a bulb and cut off about
1/4 inch from the top. Place the bulb, cut-side up, on aluminum
foil. Drizzle with olive oil, then wrap the foil around the bulb.
Bake at 400 degrees for about 30 minutes. To serve,
squeeze roasted garlic onto bread slices, discarding the peel.

Amie's Snack Roll-Ups

Cynthia Messere
Sharon, PA

*When my daughter was little, she would come home from school and
want a snack she could make all by herself. We decided these roll-ups
would be easy for her little hands to make. She experimented with many
different fillings...peanut butter & jelly or cream cheese with fruit were
the favorites. These were the first things she "cooked" all by herself.
Now, at 17 years old, she still makes them.*

12 6-inch flour tortillas
8-oz. container spreadable
   cream cheese or 1 c. creamy
   peanut butter

16-oz. pkg. frozen fruit, thawed,
   or 12-oz. jar favorite-flavor
   jam or jelly

Place a tortilla on a plate. Spread cream cheese to edges and top with
fruit, or spread with peanut butter and top with jam or jelly. Roll up to
serve. Repeat with remaining ingredients. Makes one dozen.

*Freezer jams are super-easy to make. Combine 2 cups crushed
berries with 4 cups sugar; set aside for 10 minutes. In a saucepan,
stir together a 1-3/4 ounce package of dry pectin and 3/4 cup
water. Boil for one minute, then stir into berry mixture. Let stand
3 minutes before ladling into freezer-safe containers, then
set at room temperature 30 minutes before freezing.*

Apple Wheels

Jackie Smulski
Lyons, IL

These apple wheels make a perfect little after-school snack.

1/4 c. creamy peanut butter
2 t. honey
1/2 c. semi-sweet mini chocolate
  chips

1 T. raisins
4 red or yellow apples, cored

Combine peanut butter and honey in a bowl; fold in chocolate chips and raisins. Fill centers of apples with mixture; refrigerate for one hour. Slice apples into 1/4-inch rings to serve. Makes 4 servings.

Peanut butter is a favorite with kids big and little.
When making your next snack or sandwich, try cashew
or almond butter for a yummy change.

Mom's Summer Salsa

Paula Marchesi
Lenhartsville, PA

This colorful salsa has a burst of fresh flavor in every bite. I love making it for my family each summer, and whenever I do, I'm reminded of all the good times and happy meals we've shared. It brings a good tear to my eye.

4 c. seedless watermelon, diced
1 c. green pepper, diced
1/2 c. red pepper, diced
1/2 c. orange pepper, diced
1/2 c. sweet onion, diced
1/2 c. red onion, diced
1/2 c. carrots, peeled and diced
1/2 c. celery, diced
2 jalapeño peppers, seeded and
  sliced

2 T. rice wine vinegar
1 T. oil
1 c. fresh cilantro, chopped
2 T. fresh mint, chopped
2 T. fresh basil, chopped
Garnish: 1/4 c. unsalted
  cashews, chopped

In a large bowl, combine all ingredients except cashews. Cover and refrigerate until serving. Just before serving, sprinkle with cashews. Makes 8-1/2 cups.

When buying fresh fruits & veggies, keep them farm-fresh by packing them in a cooler in your car.

All-American Sandwiches

Jo Ann

Celebrate summer with these yummy sandwiches...
the blue cheese is scrumptious!

1-1/2 T. olive oil
2 red onions, thinly sliced
3-1/2 T. red wine vinegar
6 c. arugula leaves, divided
3/4 c. mayonnaise

salt and pepper to taste
4 ciabatta rolls, halved
3/4 lb. thinly sliced smoked
  deli turkey
3/4 c. crumbled blue cheese

Heat oil in a skillet over medium-high heat. Add onions and sauté until soft and lightly golden. Remove from heat and stir in vinegar. Set aside. Chop enough arugula to equal one cup. Stir in mayonnaise; season with salt and pepper. Spread mayonnaise mixture over cut sides of rolls. Divide turkey evenly among bottom halves of rolls. Top with cheese, onion mixture, remaining arugula leaves and top halves of rolls. Makes 4 servings.

Homebaked goods are a farmers' market treat. Give new flavor to favorite sandwiches simply by trying a different type of bread. Look for a savory herb, tangy sour cream or country vegetable bread...full of flavor!

Regina's Stuffed Pitas

Regina Vining
Warwick, RI

*Pitas are a super change from buns. Try them stuffed with any
of your favorite sandwich fillings or even a crisp salad.*

1/2 lb. deli roast beef, cut into
   thin strips
2 c. romaine lettuce, shredded
1 c. carrots, peeled and
   shredded
1 c. cucumber, thinly sliced
1/2 c. red onion, thinly sliced

1/3 c. crumbled feta cheese
3 T. pine nuts, toasted
4 pita rounds, halved and split
2 T. mayonnaise
2 T. milk
1 T. cider vinegar

Stir together beef, vegetables, cheese and nuts. Spoon mixture equally
inside pita halves. Whisk remaining ingredients together. Drizzle over
pita filling. Serves 4.

*Toasting pine nuts is so easy. Place them in a dry skillet
over medium heat. Stir occasionally until lightly golden...
about 3 minutes. Cool, then add to sandwiches or salads.*

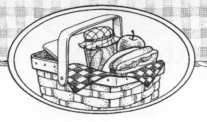

Cheesy Tuna Triangles

Barb Bargdill
Gooseberry Patch

*It's the sweet raisin bread and chopped apple that make
these sandwiches stand out from all the rest.*

1 T. oil
1 c. apple, cored and chopped
3 T. onion, chopped
7-oz. can tuna, drained
1/4 c. chopped walnuts
1/4 c. mayonnaise
2 t. lemon juice

1/8 t. salt
1/8 t. pepper
4 slices raisin bread, toasted
   and halved diagonally
4 slices sharp Cheddar cheese,
   halved diagonally

Heat oil in a skillet over medium heat; add apple and onion. Cook,
stirring occasionally, about 5 minutes until tender. Remove from heat;
transfer to a bowl. Stir in tuna, walnuts, mayonnaise, lemon juice, salt
and pepper. Place toast slices on an ungreased baking sheet. Top with
tuna mixture and a slice of cheese. Broil 4 to 5 inches from heat for
3 to 4 minutes, or until cheese begins to melt. Makes 8.

*Fill your rooms with fresh sunflowers...
they add a splash of color anywhere!*

Shrimply Wonderful Bagels

Jennifer Gubbins
Homewood, IL

Serve on mini bagels for perfect bite-size sandwiches.

3-oz. pkg. cream cheese,
  softened
4-1/4 oz. can tiny shrimp,
  drained and rinsed
2 T. mayonnaise

1 T. lemon juice
1/2 t. dill weed
4 bagels, split and toasted
1 avocado, peeled, pitted and
  sliced

Mix cream cheese, shrimp, mayonnaise, lemon juice and dill weed.
Spread mixture onto 4 bagel halves. Top with avocado slices and
remaining bagel halves. Makes 4.

It's nice to have a shopping list handy, but leave a bit of
wiggle room for foods that might be at the market early,
or something new you've never tried before. Trying new
things is part of the fun of going to farmers' markets!

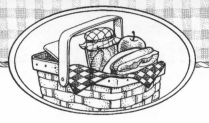

Grilled Salmon BLT's

Edie DeSpain
Logan, UT

Lemony dill mayonnaise is the secret ingredient in this recipe!

1/3 c. mayonnaise
2 t. fresh dill, chopped
1 t. lemon zest
4 1-inch-thick salmon fillets
1/4 t. salt
1/8 t. pepper

8 1/2-inch slices country-style
   bread
4 romaine lettuce leaves
2 tomatoes, sliced
6 slices bacon, crisply cooked
   and halved

Stir together mayonnaise, dill and zest; set aside. Sprinkle salmon with salt and pepper; place on a lightly greased hot grill, skin-side down. Cook, covered, about 10 to 12 minutes without turning, until cooked through. Slide a thin metal spatula between salmon and skin; lift salmon and transfer to plate. Discard skin. Arrange bread slices on grill; cook until lightly toasted on both sides. Spread mayonnaise mixture on one side of 4 toasted bread slices. Top each with one lettuce leaf, 2 tomato slices, one salmon fillet, 3 slices bacon and remaining bread slice. Makes 4.

For a scrumptious sandwich in a snap, spread cream cheese over bagels, top with snipped chives, thinly sliced cucumbers and chopped tomatoes.

Carol's Veggie Panini

Carol Lytle
Columbus, OH

A stop at a roadside market yielded a basket brimming with fresh veggies...this is the super-simple recipe I created.

2 T. balsamic vinegar
1 T. olive oil
1/2 t. salt
1/8 t. pepper
1 eggplant, cut into 1/4-inch
   slices

1 zucchini, cut into 8 slices
1 red pepper, quartered
8 slices ciabatta bread
1 c. shredded mozzarella cheese
8 fresh basil leaves

Whisk vinegar, oil, salt and pepper in a bowl; set aside. Spray a baking sheet with non-stick vegetable spray. Brush both sides of eggplant and zucchini with vinegar mixture. Arrange in a single layer on baking sheet. Coat all vegetables with vegetable spray. Broil about 4 inches from heat for 7 to 8 minutes, turning once and coating vegetables with spray as needed. Lightly brush one side of each bread slice with remaining vinegar mixture; turn and coat second side with spray. Place bread, sprayed-side down, on an ungreased baking sheet. Top with vegetables, cheese and basil. Top with remaining bread slices, sprayed-side up. Place sandwiches, one at a time, in a skillet; set a bacon press or other weight on top. Cook sandwiches over medium-high heat for about 4 minutes, turning once, until lightly golden on both sides. Makes 4 servings.

An old-fashioned picnic lunch is a terrific way to relax on a sunny afternoon. Pack sandwiches along with fresh fruits & veggies in vintage tins for easy toting.

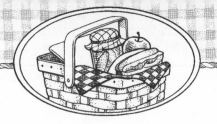

Henderson Family Gyros

Jessica Henderson
Bloomfield, IA

This recipe marinates the meat for 6 to 12 hours. The result is worth it...meat that's tender and bursting with flavor!

1/4 c. olive oil
1/4 c. dry red wine or cranberry
   juice cocktail
Optional: 1 T. vinegar
4 cloves garlic, chopped
1 T. fresh oregano, chopped

2 lbs. turkey or pork tenderloin,
   thinly sliced
6 pita rounds, split
Garnish: baby spinach, red
   onion slices, tomato slices

Combine oil, wine or juice and vinegar (only if using juice), garlic and oregano in a large plastic zipping bag. Add turkey or pork; seal and refrigerate 6 to 12 hours. Line grill surface with a piece of aluminum foil coated with non-stick vegetable spray. Heat grill to medium-high heat. Using a slotted spoon, remove meat mixture from plastic zipping bag and arrange on aluminum foil. Discard marinade. Grill and turn meat slices until browned. Drain and remove from grill. Toast pitas on grill until warmed. Spoon meat into pitas; drizzle with Cucumber Sauce. Top with desired amounts of spinach, onion and tomato. Makes 6.

Cucumber Sauce:

1/4 c. sour cream
1/4 c. cucumber, peeled and
   diced
2 T. red onion, minced

1/4 t. lemon pepper
1/4 t. dried oregano
1/8 t. garlic powder

Combine all ingredients together. Chill.

When making your favorite gyro recipe, you can swap out sour cream for plain yogurt when making the Cucumber Sauce. Try adding a drizzle of honey too. Yum!

Texas 2-Step Sandwiches

Connie Hilty
Pearland, TX

This sandwich is so good, it'll have you doing the Texas 2-step!

1 c. water
1/2 c. white wine vinegar
1 c. red onion, thinly sliced
1 c. canned black beans, drained
   and rinsed
1/2 t. ground cumin
1/4 c. mayonnaise
1 t. canned chipotle chile, finely
   chopped

1 T. lime juice
8 slices whole-grain bread
2/3 c. crumbled feta cheese
1 avocado, peeled, pitted and
   thinly sliced
2 T. fresh cilantro, chopped
1 tomato, cut into 8 slices

Pour water into a saucepan; stir in vinegar and onion. Bring to a boil; turn off heat and let stand 30 minutes. Drain. Purée beans and cumin in a blender; set side. Stir together mayonnaise, chile and juice in a bowl; spread on 4 slices of bread. Top with bean purée, onion and remaining ingredients; close sandwiches with remaining bread slices. Serves 4.

At country sales, you can often find mix & match linens,
pint-size juice glasses and retro place settings...
all will make any meal that much more fun.

Toasted Ham & Cheese

Arleela Connor
Leopold, IN

*I love to serve these sandwiches with a side of potato chips
and a crisp dill pickle. Try substituting buttermilk or
potato bread for the sourdough...they're just as tasty.*

2-1/2 T. butter
8 slices sourdough bread
1/2 lb. Colby cheese slices

1 lb. shaved deli ham
1/2 lb. Swiss cheese slices

Spread butter on one side of each slice of bread. Arrange 4 bread
slices, buttered-side down, on a grill over medium-high heat. Top with
one slice Colby cheese, desired amount of ham and one slice Swiss
cheese. Add remaining bread slices, buttered-side up. Grill sandwiches
on both sides, until golden and cheese is melted. Serves 4.

Markets often have blackboards listing the prices for their
fresh produce or baked goods. Make your own blackboard for
home...it's easy. Coat a flat surface with chalkboard paint;
let dry, then recoat. Turn cast-off cabinet doors, a salvaged
mirror or old window into a handy kitchen blackboard!

Turkey & Berry Sandwiches

Kim Hinshaw
Austin, TX

I served these sandwiches to several friends while we were vacationing at the beach. Truly...everyone raved and requested the recipe!

2 lettuce leaves
2 slices Swiss cheese
1/4 lb. thinly sliced deli turkey
4 strawberries, hulled and sliced

4 slices whole-wheat bread
2 T. whipped cream cheese
  spread
2 t. pecans, finely chopped

Layer lettuce, cheese, turkey and strawberries on 2 slices of bread. Combine cream cheese and pecans. Spread over remaining bread slices; close sandwiches. Serves 2.

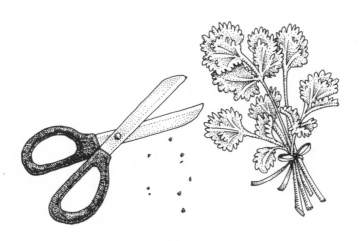

For a quick & easy chicken salad recipe, combine shredded deli chicken with snipped fresh cilantro, lime juice, halved grapes, chopped red onion and mayonnaise to taste.

Amish Peanut Butter Spread

Jennie Wiseman
Coshocton, OH

Spread over slices of homemade bread, this is a favorite of Amish families...it will be in your family, too!

3/8 c. corn syrup
5 c. brown sugar, packed
2-1/2 c. hot water
1 t. vanilla extract

40-oz. jar creamy peanut butter
3 lbs. marshmallow creme
6 1-pint plastic containers and
   lids, sterilized

Combine corn syrup, brown sugar and water in a saucepan; bring to a boil over medium heat. Remove from heat and cool completely. Stir in remaining ingredients. Spoon into a 3-quart container and cover; refrigerate overnight. Bring to room temperature. Spoon into airtight containers leaving 1/2-inch headspace. Store in refrigerator. Makes 6 containers.

Baskets come in all shapes and sizes and are roomy for holding bunches of market-fresh veggies or apples from the orchard. Stitch up pretty liners from scraps of ticking or tea towels...super easy.

Strawberry Patch Sandwich

Shelley Turner
Boise, ID

Try the banana bread...it's oh-so yummy
paired with peanut butter and strawberries.

2 slices whole-wheat bread or
   banana bread
1 T. creamy peanut butter

1 T. cream cheese, softened
2 strawberries, hulled and sliced
1 t. honey

Spread one slice of bread with peanut butter. Spread remaining slice with cream cheese. Arrange strawberry slices in a single layer over peanut butter. Drizzle honey over berries; close sandwich. Makes one serving.

Once the yummy jams & jellies have been enjoyed,
canning jars are ideal for keeping fun crafty items at
your fingertips. Fill jars with snippets of ribbon,
vintage buttons, tags, trims and rick rack.

Herb Garden Sandwiches

Lynda Robson
Boston, MA

*Just outside our back door is a kitchen garden filled with fresh herbs.
One sunny afternoon my daughter and I whipped up these
sandwiches to take to a church picnic...we think they're terrific!*

8-oz. pkg. cream cheese,
   softened
1 t. lemon juice
1/8 t. hot pepper sauce
1/2 c. fresh herbs, finely
   chopped, such as parsley,
   watercress, basil, chervil,
   chives

8 slices whole-wheat bread,
   crusts removed
paprika to taste

Combine all ingredients except bread and paprika. Spread mixture
evenly over each bread slice. Sprinkle with paprika. Close sandwiches;
slice diagonally into quarters. Makes 16.

Asparagus bundles are a great go-with for sandwiches.
Steam trimmed asparagus until it's crisp-tender, then transfer
to a bowl of ice water to cool. Drain, and bundle 6 spears
together and tie with fresh chive stems. Drizzle with
your favorite vinaigrette...so easy!

Dilly Chicken Sandwiches

Rebecca Billington
Birmingham, AL

This is a great sandwich to make for a family get-together.
We always add several bread & butter pickles to our sandwiches...
we think they make the sandwich taste even better!

4 boneless, skinless chicken
  breasts
6 T. butter, softened and divided
1 clove garlic, minced
3/4 t. dill weed, divided

8 slices French bread
4 T. cream cheese, softened
2 t. lemon juice
Garnish: lettuce leaves, tomato
  slices, bread & butter pickles

Place one chicken breast between 2 pieces of wax paper. Using a mallet, flatten to 1/4-inch thickness. Repeat with remaining chicken; set aside. In a skillet over medium-high heat, melt 3 tablespoons butter; stir in garlic and 1/2 teaspoon dill weed. Add chicken; cook on both sides until juices run clear. Remove and keep warm. Spread both sides of bread with remaining butter. In a skillet or griddle, grill bread on both sides until golden. Combine remaining ingredients except garnish, and spread on one side of 4 slices grilled bread. Top with chicken; garnish as desired. Top with remaining bread. Makes 4.

A salad of fresh green beans is so delicious! Try tossing them
with chopped garlic, snipped chives, sugar snap peas
and crisply cooked and crumbled bacon.

Town Square Favorite

Tiffany Brinkley
Broomfield, CO

A visit with friends for the weekend took us to a terrific farmers' market on the town square. We filled our baskets to overflowing with veggies, herbs, sunflowers, even cheese...what a day! That same day, we made these yummy open-faced sandwiches for dinner.

3 T. butter
1-1/2 c. sliced mushrooms
1/2 c. red onion, sliced and
   separated into rings
2 zucchini, thinly sliced
1 t. dried basil
1/2 t. garlic, finely chopped
1/4 t. salt
1/4 t. pepper
4 bagels, split
8-oz. pkg. shredded Monterey
   Jack cheese, divided
2 tomatoes, sliced

Melt butter in a skillet over medium heat. Stir in all ingredients except bagels, cheese and tomatoes. Cook, stirring occasionally, until vegetables are crisp-tender, about 4 to 5 minutes. Arrange bagels on an ungreased baking sheet. Sprinkle 1/4 cup cheese over each bagel half. Bake at 375 degrees for 5 minutes, or until cheese is melted. Remove from oven; top each with one slice tomato. Spoon on vegetable mixture; top with remaining cheese. Continue baking 4 to 5 minutes longer, or until cheese is melted. Makes 4 servings.

While there are armloads of garden-fresh produce at the farmers' market, you'll also find honey, bread, cheese, flavored oils and vinegars, cookies, jams and preserves.

Suzanne's Tomato Melt

Audrey Lett
Newark, DE

I love this as a quick snack, and it's so simple to make.

1/4 c. shredded Cheddar cheese
1 onion bagel or English muffin,
  split

2 tomato slices
1 T. shredded Parmesan cheese

Sprinkle half the Cheddar cheese over each bagel or English muffin half. Top with a tomato slice. Sprinkle half the Parmesan cheese over each tomato. Broil about 6 inches from heat for 4 to 5 minutes, or until cheese is bubbly. Makes one serving.

There's just something about the flavor of summertime
tomatoes...they are the absolute best. To enjoy that fresh
taste year 'round, pick up a tomato press. It easily seeds and
peels tomatoes with the turn of a handle. Tomatoes can
then be added to favorite sauce or salsa recipes
for canning or freezing. It's so easy!

Market Veggie Triangles

Wendy Lee Paffenroth
Pine Island, NY

*Come home with your basket of veggies from the
farmers' market for these tasty sandwiches.*

2 to 3 cucumbers, chopped
8-oz. pkg. cream cheese,
  softened
1/4 c. mayonnaise
1 T. lemon juice
1/8 t. hot pepper sauce
1/2 c. red pepper, chopped
1/4 c. onion, finely chopped

1/4 c. green olives with
  pimentos, finely chopped
1 T. fresh parsley, chopped
salt and pepper to taste
12 slices wheat or pumpernickel
  bread, crusts trimmed
Garnish: green olive or
  cucumber slices

Place cucumbers in a strainer for 15 to 20 minutes to allow liquid to
drain. Combine remaining ingredients except bread and garnish in a
bowl. Stir until well blended. Add drained cucumbers; stir again.
Refrigerate, covered, for 2 to 3 hours. Slice bread into triangles.
Spread with cucumber mixture. Garnish as desired. Makes 4 dozen.

*Bringing home herb and flower plants is such fun...and so
is finding clever containers to plant them in. Auctions
and barn sales turn up some of the best planters...
old gardening boots, washtubs, enamelware pots
& pans, even tea kettles and coffeepots!*

Tangy Radish Sandwiches

Zoe Bennett
Columbia, SC

A blend of ginger and chives with a little kick of radish...
these sandwiches are really good!

4 T. butter, softened
3 T. fresh chives, chopped and
　divided
1 T. toasted sesame seed
3/4 t. fresh ginger, peeled and
　grated

1/4 t. sesame oil
salt and pepper to taste
1 baguette, sliced 1/4-inch thick
10 radishes, thinly sliced

Mix butter, 2 tablespoons chives, sesame seed, ginger and oil in a
bowl. Sprinkle with salt and pepper. Spread mixture over one side of
each baguette slice. Top with radishes, overlapping slightly. Sprinkle
with remaining chives. Makes 16 servings.

*A wire basket once used for canning jars is easily turned into
a silverware caddy. Mason jars can be filled with silverware,
while a thermos of blooms sits nicely in the middle.*

Toasted Green Tomato Sandwiches

Janie Reed
Gooseberry Patch

When my son requested these sandwiches a second time,
I realized I'd "hit the mark"!

1-1/2 to 2 c. cornmeal
salt, pepper and seasoning salt
   to taste
2 green tomatoes, sliced
   1/4-inch thick

oil or shortening for frying
2 to 3 T. butter, softened
8 slices whole-wheat bread

Combine cornmeal and seasonings in a large plastic zipping bag. Shake to mix well. Add tomato slices and gently shake to coat. Remove from bag, shaking off excess cornmeal mixture. Heat oil or shortening in a large skillet over medium heat; fry tomatoes until golden on both sides. Remove from skillet. Spread butter on one side of each slice. Arrange 4 slices, butter-side down, in skillet. Top with tomato slices and remaining bread, butter-side up. Cook over medium heat, turning once, until golden on both sides. Serves 4.

Try making fried red tomatoes...
a scrumptious twist on the expected green tomatoes.

Red Pepper & Chicken Bagels

Janice Pigga
Bethlehem, PA

This is a quick recipe that's perfect whenever time is short.

2 boneless, skinless chicken
   breasts
1/8 t. salt
1/8 t. pepper
1/4 c. balsamic vinegar

3 T. Worcestershire sauce
2 bagels, split
2 slices fresh mozzarella cheese
2 slices roasted red pepper

Place chicken between 2 pieces of wax paper; pound until thin.
Sprinkle with salt and pepper. In a bowl, combine vinegar and
Worcestershire sauce; marinate chicken 10 to 15 minutes. Drain
and discard marinade. Place chicken on a lightly greased grill or in a
skillet over medium heat. Cook and turn chicken until golden and
juices run clear, about 20 minutes. Place chicken on bagel halves; top
with cheese, pepper slices and remaining bagel halves. Arrange on an
ungreased baking sheet and bake at 350 degrees until cheese is
melted, about 5 to 10 minutes. Serves 2.

Often a flat of flowers, veggies or herbs is more than you need.
Check with family & friends to see if they'd like to swap. It's fun
to pass along plants and create your own friendship garden.

Ranch BLT Wraps

Rachel Dingler
Howell, MI

Our family loves to enjoy these wraps with a bowl of soup.

6 leaves green leaf lettuce
6 sandwich wraps
12-oz. pkg. bacon, crisply
   cooked

1 lb. boneless, skinless chicken
   breasts, cooked and cubed
2 tomatoes, diced
ranch salad dressing to taste

Place one leaf lettuce on each sandwich wrap. Top with 2 to 3 slices bacon. Spoon chicken and tomatoes evenly over bacon. Drizzle with salad dressing and roll up. Makes 6.

An old-fashioned wire egg basket makes a handy farmers' market tote. When it's not in use for that, mount it on the garden shed wall as a handy spot to store bulbs or garden tools.

Susan's Chicken Minis

Susan Brzozowski
Ellicott City, MD

I was trying to think of something a little different for lunch when I created these mini sandwiches. Now they're a favorite!

2 T. lemon juice
1/2 c. mayonnaise
salt to taste
1 t. pepper
3-1/2 c. cooked chicken, finely
   diced

1/2 c. celery, finely diced
1/3 c. raisins
1/3 c. chopped walnuts
12 mini dinner rolls, split

Combine lemon juice, mayonnaise, salt and pepper. Toss with remaining ingredients except rolls. Spoon mixture onto rolls. Makes 12 mini sandwiches.

While most farmers' markets are open on Saturday mornings, check to see if your area has a smaller mid-week market on Wednesday or Thursday evenings. There are even fall and winter farmers' markets popping up in some towns.

Raspberry-Dijon Baguettes

Deborah Lomax
Peoria, IL

A friend shared a similar recipe using roast beef...
this is my spin on that recipe using grilled chicken.

1 baguette, sliced
Dijon mustard and raspberry
   jam to taste
4 boneless, skinless chicken
   breasts, grilled and sliced

2 c. arugula leaves
Optional: red onion slices

Spread 4 slices of baguette with mustard. Top remaining slices with raspberry jam. Arrange a layer of grilled chicken over mustard; top with arugula and onion, if desired. Top with remaining baguette slices. Serves 4.

Transform a vintage vent cover into a terrific recipe sorter.
Find a vent with a back flap that can become a stand when
it's pulled out. Then, with a little cleaning and a fresh coat
of paint, it's ready to hold your favorite recipe cards.

Aunt Betty's Sandwiches

Geneva Rogers
Gillette, WY

As kids, our summertime drive to Aunt Betty's was always a long-awaited treat. Although it was a long drive, we'd stop along the way, stretch our legs, then hop back in the car. When we finally arrived, Aunt Betty would greet us at the door all smiles and in her favorite apron. She knew we'd be hungry, and these sandwiches were always waiting for us.

4 ciabatta rolls
3 T. olive oil, divided, plus more
   for drizzling
whole-grain mustard to taste
1/2 lb. fontina cheese, shredded
   and divided

12-oz. pkg. sliced mushrooms
2 T. shallots, chopped
3 cloves garlic, pressed
2 c. deli roast chicken, shredded
5-oz. pkg. baby spinach
salt and pepper to taste

Slice tops from rolls; set aside. Hollow out each roll; drizzle inside of each with oil. Spread inside of each roll with mustard; sprinkle with half the cheese. Heat 2 tablespoons remaining oil in a skillet over medium-high heat. Add mushrooms; sauté until tender. Stir in shallots and garlic; cook and stir about 3 minutes. Add chicken; continue cooking until heated through. Transfer to a plate and keep warm. Add remaining oil to skillet. Stir in spinach and season with salt and pepper. Cook about 2 minutes; drain. Spoon chicken mixture into rolls; top with spinach. Sprinkle each with remaining cheese. Cover with tops of rolls and wrap each tightly in aluminum foil. Bake at 400 degrees about 20 minutes, or until cheese is melted. Serves 4.

I have several acres about my house which I call my garden, and which a skilled gardener would not know what to call.
   -Joseph Addison

Egg Salad Minis

Jennifer Niemi
Nova Scotia, Canada

Farm-fresh eggs are a farmers' market treat...don't pass them up!

4 eggs, hard-boiled, peeled and
　chopped
1/4 c. onion, finely chopped
mayonnaise to taste, divided

salt and pepper to taste
butter to taste, softened
14 slices soft sandwich bread,
　crusts removed

Using a fork, mash eggs. Stir in onion. Add mayonnaise and seasoning to taste. Spread butter on half the bread slices and spread mayonnaise on remaining bread slices. Spoon on egg mixture. Top with remaining bread and cut diagonally in quarters. Makes 28 mini sandwiches.

Whip up a refreshing watermelon slush...a snap to make in a blender. Combine 3 cups diced watermelon, 2 tablespoons lime juice, one tablespoon sugar, one cup crushed ice and 1/2 cup water. Blend until combined, but still slushy.

82

Pie-Iron Tomato Sandwiches

Samantha Sparks
Madison, WI

Perfect for a quick & easy dinner around a fire pit or campfire.

12 to 16 slices bread
1/4 c. butter, softened
4 tomatoes, sliced

2 onions, sliced
salt and pepper to taste

Spread bread slices with butter; top half of the slices with tomatoes and onions. Sprinkle with salt and pepper to taste. Top with remaining bread slices, buttered-side up. Place sandwiches in an ungreased pie iron and place on coals until toasted, about 4 to 6 minutes. Makes 6 to 8 sandwiches.

Remember not to refrigerate fresh tomatoes...
they'll keep their just-picked taste longer stored
on your cupboard shelf or counter.

Roasted Veggie Rolls

Becky Tetlak
Mountain Top, PA

Here's a super recipe for your bushel of zucchini!

2 portabella mushroom caps
1 zucchini, thinly sliced
1 tomato, sliced
6-oz. jar artichoke hearts,
   drained
1 clove garlic, minced

1 T. olive oil
1/2 t. lemon juice
1/8 t. kosher salt
pepper to taste
2 multi-grain rolls, split
1/4 c. crumbled feta cheese

Arrange mushrooms and zucchini on a greased baking sheet. Bake at 400 degrees for 10 minutes. Add tomato to the baking sheet and continue baking 15 minutes longer, turning vegetables halfway through baking time. In a food processor, combine remaining ingredients except rolls and cheese; pulse to blend. Spread artichoke mixture over split rolls; layer with vegetables and cheese. Makes 2 servings.

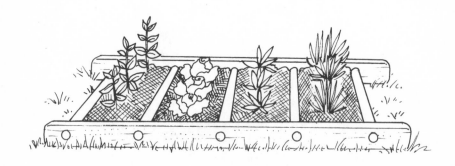

Lay a wooden ladder flat on the ground and fill the open spaces with potting soil to create a clever raised bed. The small-size spaces are just right for growing herbs and lettuces.

Mediterranean Sandwiches

Shirl Parsons
Cape Carteret, NC

This is a tasty twist on the "usual" chicken salad sandwich.

4 boneless, skinless chicken
    breasts
1 t. dried basil
1/4 t. salt
1/4 t. pepper
1 c. cucumber, chopped
1/2 c. mayonnaise
1/4 c. roasted red pepper,
    chopped

1/4 c. sliced black olives
1/4 c. plain yogurt
1/4 t. garlic powder
6 kaiser rolls, split
Garnish: mayonnaise, lettuce
    leaves

Combine chicken, basil, salt and pepper in a stockpot. Cover with
water and bring to a boil. Reduce heat and simmer, covered, 10 to
12 minutes until chicken is no longer pink in center. Remove chicken
from pan; set aside to cool. Cube chicken and combine with remaining
ingredients except rolls and garnish. Toss well to coat. Spread rolls
with additional mayonnaise; top with lettuce and chicken salad
mixture. Makes 6 servings.

Kay's Bacon-Tomato Sandwiches

Cheryl Lagler
Zionsville, PA

When my children were young, my friend Kay and I would get together monthly to visit and have lunch. Kay first prepared this sandwich and I knew I had a quick & delicious dinner recipe for my family. The flavors blend together in a truly scrumptious sandwich!

1/3 c. mayonnaise
1 T. mustard
4 onion rolls, split
8 slices bacon, crisply cooked

4 slices tomato
12 slices red onion
12 slices cucumber
8 slices Cheddar cheese

Combine mayonnaise and mustard; spread evenly over cut side of rolls. Layer remaining ingredients on rolls in order given. Close sandwiches and place on an ungreased baking sheet. Bake at 350 degrees for 5 to 8 minutes, or until cheese melts. Makes 4.

For a delightful fragrance, save and dry lavender flowers, then spoon into a sweetly stitched square of vintage-y fabric.

Apricot Chicken Sandwiches

Anna McMaster
Portland, OR

I usually toss grape halves or raisins in my chicken salad,
but this is one time I tried something new. It tastes terrific!

4 c. cooked chicken, diced
1 stalk celery, finely diced
2 T. onion, finely chopped
3 apricots, pitted and finely
   diced

mayonnaise to taste
salt and pepper to taste
4 pita rounds, halved

Combine chicken, celery, onion and apricots. Stir in mayonnaise;
season to taste. Spoon into pita halves. Serves 4.

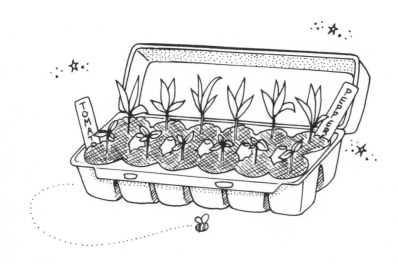

Cardboard egg cartons make perfect seed-starting
flats. Fill with potting soil and seeds, and when
it's time to plant, separate the sections
and tuck each into the soil.

Aloha Sandwiches

Kaylene Duncan
Churubusco, IN

This sandwich couldn't be any easier to prepare...
just toss together all the ingredients!

3 10-oz. cans chicken, drained
1 c. celery, chopped
1 c. mayonnaise-type salad
   dressing
1 c. seedless grapes, halved

1/4 c. whipping cream
1/2 c. chopped pecans
1 t. salt
12-oz. pkg. Hawaiian rolls, split

Combine all ingredients except salt and rolls. Sprinkle with salt, blend well and spoon over rolls. Serves 4 to 8.

Keep a jar of sweet Honey-Mustard Butter on hand for
sandwiches...everyone will love it. Combine 4 tablespoons
honey and 4 tablespoons Dijon mustard with one cup
softened butter, blending until smooth.

A Bushel Basket of Main Dishes

Easy Fettuccine Primavera

Patricia Wissler
Harrisburg, PA

This is a great recipe for fresh veggies. So simple,
it can easily be prepared even on a busy night.

12-oz. pkg. fettuccine pasta,
  cooked
1/2 c. creamy Italian salad
  dressing
1 c. broccoli flowerets
1 c. zucchini, sliced
1 c. red peppers, thinly sliced

1/2 c. onion, chopped
1/2 t. dried basil
1/2 c. butter
2 tomatoes, chopped
1/2 c. sliced mushrooms
Garnish: grated Parmesan
  cheese

Toss warm pasta with salad dressing; stir to coat. Set aside; cover to
keep warm. In a skillet over medium heat, cook broccoli, zucchini,
peppers, onion and basil in butter until tender. Stir in tomatoes and
mushrooms; cook just until heated through. Toss vegetable mixture
with warm pasta. Garnish with Parmesan cheese. Serves 6.

Trying a different type of pasta will give every meal a
tasty change. Whole-wheat, spinach and pesto flavors
are delicious in any of your favorite recipes.

Angie's Pasta & Sauce

Angie Whitmore
Farmington, UT

*Homemade sauce is so simple to prepare. You'll love the taste
of both the sauce and the freshly grated Parmesan on top.*

6 to 8 roma tomatoes, halved,
   seeded and diced
1 to 2 cloves garlic, minced
1/2 c. butter, melted
1 T. dried basil

8-oz. pkg. angel hair pasta,
   cooked
Garnish: freshly grated
   Parmesan cheese

Combine tomatoes and garlic in a saucepan. Simmer over medium
heat 15 minutes; set aside. Blend together butter and basil; add to
pasta. Toss to coat. Stir in tomato mixture and garnish. Serves 4 to 6.

A vintage enamelware cup easily becomes a whimsical candle
for picnics on the porch. Use melted beeswax and a wick...
craft stores sell all the supplies and instructions you'll need.
Remember to place candles on a safe surface for burning.

Vegetable Patch Pot Pie

Megan Brooks
Antioch, TN

The flavors of fresh veggies really make this recipe a stand-out.
A summertime trip to the farmers' market or a visit to a roadside
stand will send you home with everything you need.

1 onion, chopped
8-oz. pkg. sliced mushrooms
1 clove garlic, minced
2 T. olive oil
2 carrots, peeled and diced
2 potatoes, peeled and diced
2 stalks celery, sliced
2 c. cauliflower flowerets
1 c. green beans, trimmed and
    snapped into 1/2-inch pieces

3 c. vegetable broth
1 t. kosher salt
1 t. pepper
2 T. cornstarch
2 T. soy sauce
1/4 c. water
2 pie crusts

In a skillet over medium heat, cook onion, mushrooms and garlic in oil for 3 to 5 minutes. Stir frequently. Stir in remaining vegetables and broth. Bring to a boil; reduce heat and simmer. Cook until vegetables are just tender, about 5 minutes. Season with salt and pepper. In a small bowl, combine cornstarch, soy sauce and water. Mix until cornstarch has dissolved. Stir mixture into vegetables; simmer until sauce thickens. Roll out one crust and place in an ungreased 11"x7" baking pan. Spoon filling evenly over pastry. Roll out remaining crust and arrange over filling; crimp edges. Bake at 425 degrees for 30 minutes, or until crust is golden. Makes 6 servings.

Farmers' markets have oodles
of fresh fruits & veggies along
with herbs and perennials.
Tuck Hens & Chicks or
herbs into metal colanders,
farm buckets, little wagons
and wooden crates...the
possibilities are endless!

Garlicky Chicken & Redskin Potatoes   *Vickie*

*Our market runs from May through the end of October. Vendors have
tables filled with fresh baked goods, flowers, fruit, veggies, herbs,
perennials and honey. There's something for everyone!*

8 chicken breasts
3 lbs. redskin potatoes, halved
20 cloves garlic, peeled
1 T. fresh thyme, chopped

salt and pepper to taste
1/4 c. olive oil
Optional: fresh thyme sprigs

Place chicken in an ungreased roasting pan. Arrange potatoes and
garlic around chicken. Sprinkle with seasonings and drizzle with oil.
Bake uncovered at 425 degrees for 20 minutes. Reduce oven
temperature to 375 degrees. Continue baking 45 minutes to one hour,
or until chicken is golden and juices run clear. Transfer chicken to a
platter. Spoon potatoes and garlic around edges. Garnish with thyme
sprigs, if desired. Serves 8.

*While you're at the farmers' market, pick up a garlic bulb
to plant in your own garden. (Don't use regular supermarket
garlic which was probably treated with a sprouting inhibitor.)
Plant individual cloves 2 inches deep and one foot apart.
When flower stalks begin to appear, cut them back. About
midsummer, the leaves will begin to turn yellow...
dig up your garlic and enjoy!*

Creamy Pesto & Bowties

Cherylann Smith
Efland, NC

My kids love this!

1 lb. boneless, skinless chicken
    breasts
2 T. butter
8-oz. pkg. bowtie pasta,
    uncooked and divided

10-3/4 oz. can cream of celery
    soup
1/2 c. pesto sauce
1/2 c. milk

In a skillet over medium heat, cook chicken in butter until golden and juices run clear. Meanwhile, cook 3 cups pasta according to package directions; reserve remaining pasta for another recipe. Set aside and cover to keep warm. Stir remaining ingredients into chicken; bring to a boil. Reduce heat and simmer 5 minutes. Stir in pasta and heat through. Serves 4.

Try making pesto at home...it's so fresh and flavorful!
Toss together one bunch finely chopped fresh basil,
3 cloves minced garlic, 3/4 cup freshly grated Parmesan
cheese and 3 tablespoons pine nuts. Drizzle with
3 to 4 tablespoons olive oil; stir to blend.

Zucchini & Ratatouille Pasta

Jennifer Breeden
Chesterfield, VA

This recipe makes it easy to use some of those wonderful garden veggies...it's good for you too!

2 T. olive oil
3/4 lb. boneless, skinless
  chicken breasts, cut into
  1/2-inch pieces
1 c. green pepper, sliced
1-1/2 c. eggplant, peeled and
  diced

1-1/2 c. zucchini, thinly sliced
27-1/2 oz. jar pasta sauce
8-oz. pkg. penne pasta, cooked
Garnish: grated Parmesan
  cheese

Heat oil in a saucepan over medium-high heat; add chicken and pepper. Cook, stirring frequently, until chicken is no longer pink. Add eggplant and zucchini; cook 3 minutes, stirring frequently, until vegetables are tender. Stir in pasta sauce and heat to boiling. Reduce heat and simmer, uncovered, 10 minutes or until chicken juices run clear. Spoon sauce over pasta and sprinkle with Parmesan cheese. Serves 6.

As soon as you're home from the market, rinse fruits & veggies, then jot down menu ideas. This way, you'll enjoy them at their very freshest.

Roberta's Pepper Steak

Roberta Goll
Chesterfield, MI

A time-tested favorite...and so simple to prepare.

2 lbs. beef round steak, sliced
   into 1/2-inch strips
2 T. olive oil
2 cloves garlic, pressed and
   divided
2 green peppers, cut into thin
   strips

2 onions, coarsely chopped
8-oz. pkg. sliced mushrooms
2 t. salt
1/2 t. pepper
3/4 c. red wine or beef broth
1/4 t. to 1/2 t. curry powder
chicken broth, as needed

In a skillet over medium heat, brown steak strips with oil and half the garlic. Add peppers and onions; cook until tender. Stir in mushrooms, salt, pepper and remaining garlic. Stir in wine or beef broth. Reduce heat to low and simmer for 30 minutes. Sprinkle with curry powder and continue simmering one hour. Add chicken broth as needed to prevent sticking and overbrowning. Serves 6 to 8.

To dig and delve in nice clean dirt
can do a mortal little hurt.
-John Kendrick Banks

Preference Dinner

Wendy Jacobs
Idaho Falls, ID

While in college, there was a yearly dance called Preference...at this dance, the ladies invited the men. This was the dinner I prepared for my date. My cooking must not have been too bad...we've been married now for many years!

juice of 1 lime
salt and pepper to taste
1-1/2 lb. beef flank steak
1/2 bunch broccoli, cut into
   flowerets

2 c. baby carrots, sliced
2 ears corn, husked and cut into
   2-inch pieces
1 red onion, sliced into wedges
2 T. olive oil

Combine lime juice, salt and pepper; brush over both sides of beef. Place on a broiler pan and broil, 5 minutes per side, turning once. Set aside on a cutting board; keep warm. Toss broccoli, carrots, corn and onion with oil. Spoon onto a lightly greased baking sheet in a single layer. Bake at 475 degrees, turning once, until cooked through, about 10 minutes. Slice steak into thin strips and arrange on a platter. Surround with vegetables. Serves 4 to 6.

Kitchen tea towels are a must for drying just-rinsed garden vegetables. Practical and pretty, you'll want to keep several on hand.

Chicken-Broccoli Roll

Diane Williams
Mountain Top, PA

*I make this ahead of time when my daughter is
coming home from college for the weekend.*

2 c. cooked chicken, diced
1 c. broccoli, chopped
1/2 c. red pepper, chopped
1 t. garlic powder
1 c. shredded Cheddar cheese
1/2 c. mayonnaise

2 t. dill weed
1/4 t. salt
2 8-oz. tubes refrigerated
   crescent rolls

Combine chicken, broccoli, pepper and garlic powder; set aside. In a
separate bowl, combine remaining ingredients except crescent rolls;
add to chicken mixture. Unroll crescent roll dough and place side-by-
side on a baking sheet that has been lightly sprayed with non-stick
vegetable spray. Pinch seams together. Spoon chicken mixture down
the center of dough. Bring up sides and fold over chicken; pinch
seams and ends to seal. Bake at 350 degrees for 25 to 28 minutes,
until golden. Serves 4.

*Letters from an old board game look so fun when
glued together to make words. Use them to spell out
"potatoes" and "onions" and hang over veggie bins.*

98

Asparagus Shepherd's Pie

Kathy Reichert
Meridian, ID

*Adding fresh asparagus to this familiar recipe
really gives it a tasty spin.*

6 potatoes, peeled and quartered
1 lb. ground beef
1 onion, chopped
2 cloves garlic, minced
10-3/4 oz. can cream of
   asparagus soup
1/4 t. pepper
1 lb. asparagus, trimmed and
   cut into 1-inch pieces

1/2 c. milk
1/4 c. butter or margarine
1 t. dried sage
3/4 t. salt
1/2 c. shredded mozzarella
   cheese
paprika to taste

Add potatoes to a saucepan; cover with water. Cook over medium heat until tender. Drain and set aside; cover to keep warm. Brown beef in a skillet over medium heat; drain. Add onion and garlic; cook until tender. Stir in soup and pepper. Pour mixture into a greased 2-quart dish. Cook asparagus in a small amount of water over medium heat until crisp-tender, about 3 to 4 minutes. Drain and arrange over beef mixture. Mash potatoes with milk, butter, sage and salt. Spread over asparagus. Sprinkle with cheese and paprika. Bake, uncovered, at 350 degrees for 20 minutes. Makes 4 to 6 servings.

*Instead of one large flower bouquet centerpiece, set a
single zinnia flower bloom in white milk glass
cups for each place setting. Oh-so pretty.*

Basil & Tomato Halibut

Debra Van Zant.
Stevenson Ranch, CA

Slices of garden-fresh tomatoes and a sprinkle of freshly chopped basil taste amazing spooned over servings of fish.

1 onion, sliced
4 cloves garlic, minced
1 T. olive oil
1 t. butter
8 roma tomatoes, diced
14-1/2 oz. can chicken broth

1 t. seafood seasoning
salt and pepper to taste
2 lbs. halibut fillets
cooked rice
fresh basil to taste, chopped

In a skillet over medium heat, sauté onion and garlic in oil and butter for 3 minutes. Stir in tomatoes, broth and seasonings. Add fish to skillet. Cook, covered, over medium heat until fish flakes easily, about 8 minutes. Remove fish from sauce and lay on a bed of rice. Add basil to sauce; stir and spoon over fish and rice. Makes 4 to 6 servings.

*Fresh corn on the cob is always a favorite summer side dish.
Make buttering ears a snap...add melted butter to
a glass tall enough for dipping ears of corn.*

Italian Orange Roughy

Mary Gage
Wakewood, CA

*Once marinated, this microwave dinner is ready
in under 10 minutes!*

1 lb. orange roughy fillets
1/2 c. tomato juice
2 T. white vinegar
.7-oz. pkg. Italian salad
   dressing mix

1/4 c. green onions, chopped
1/4 c. green pepper, chopped

Place fish fillets in a shallow 2-quart microwave-safe dish. Combine tomato juice, vinegar and salad dressing mix. Pour over fish. Cover and refrigerate for 30 minutes. Uncover; sprinkle with onions and pepper. Microwave, covered, on high for 3 minutes. Turn fish, cover again and cook 2 to 4 minutes longer, until fish flakes easily. Let stand for 2 minutes before uncovering. Serves 4.

*For a quick & easy side salad, toss cool cucumber slices
with leafy greens and crumbled cheese...
drizzle with oil & vinegar.*

Susan's Vegetable Lasagna

Susan Province
Strawberry Plains, TN

*I created this recipe for my family as a way to add more fresh
vegetables to our meals. It's really versatile...use any fresh
veggies that are in season, or substitute frozen if necessary.*

2 t. olive oil
6 c. vegetables, diced, such as
  zucchini, yellow squash,
  carrots, broccoli, red pepper,
  mushrooms
1 onion, diced
2 cloves garlic, minced
2 to 6 T. soy sauce or
  Worcestershire sauce
pepper to taste
1/2 t. dried basil

1/2 t. dried oregano
26-oz. jar marinara sauce,
  divided
9-oz. pkg. no-boil lasagna
  noodles, uncooked and
  divided
1 c. ricotta cheese
1 c. grated Parmesan cheese
1-1/2 c. shredded mozzarella
  cheese

Over medium-high heat, drizzle oil into a skillet. Add vegetables and
onion; stir-fry until onion turns translucent. Add garlic and soy sauce
or Worcestershire sauce; continue cooking until vegetables are tender.
Season with pepper, basil and oregano. Spoon 1/2 cup sauce into an
ungreased 13"x9" baking pan. Arrange 1/3 of the noodles on the
bottom; spoon on half the ricotta cheese and half the Parmesan
cheese. Top with half of the vegetables. Repeat again, ending with
remaining noodles. Pour on the remaining sauce and sprinkle with
mozzarella cheese. Bake, uncovered, at 350 degrees for 25 to
30 minutes. Serves 8.

*Create a lasagna garden right outside the kitchen door!
Plant onions, garlic, basil, oregano, roma tomatoes and
any of your favorite veggies. When harvest season
comes, you'll have a fabulous feast!*

Bruschetta Pizza

Madonna Alexander
Chicago, IL

If you can, prepare the bruschetta mix early in the day. The longer the flavor blends, the better it tastes. You'll have some left over but that's okay. I made an omelet with this mix and it was awesome!

10 roma tomatoes, chopped
5 to 6 cloves garlic, minced
2 T. fresh basil, chopped
1/2 red onion, finely chopped
1/4 c. plus 1 T. olive oil, divided
1/2 t. pepper
1/4 t. garlic salt
1/4 c. balsamic vinegar
13.8-oz. tube refrigerated pizza crust dough
1/2 c. pizza sauce
8-oz. pkg. shredded Italian-blend cheese
dried oregano to taste

In a large bowl, combine tomatoes, garlic, basil, onion, 1/4 cup oil, pepper, garlic salt and vinegar. Stir to blend; drain. Place pizza crust dough on an ungreased baking sheet. Spread with pizza sauce. Top with 1-1/2 to 2 cups tomato mixture. Sprinkle on cheese and oregano. Drizzle remaining oil over top. Bake according to pizza crust dough package directions. Serves 6.

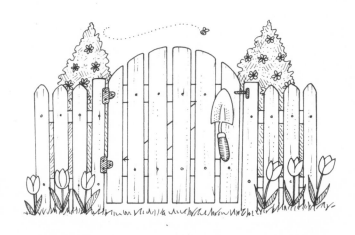

Spruce up garden gates and doors with handles made from spades or trowels. How clever!

Anytime Tortellini

Patricia Guerard
Hillsborough, NJ

A dish you really can enjoy anytime...either lunch or dinner.
For a lighter meal, use angel hair pasta in place of the tortellini.

1 T. olive oil
2 boneless, skinless chicken
   breasts
1 t. Montreal seasoning for
   chicken, divided
1 lb. asparagus, sliced into
   1-inch pieces
1 portabella mushroom cap,
   chopped
6 pieces sun-dried tomatoes,
   minced
1 T. dried parsley

salt to taste
1 T. Italian seasoning
1 c. white Zinfandel wine or
   chicken broth
2 16-oz. pkgs. cheese or meat
   tortellini, uncooked
2 14-1/2 oz. cans diced
   tomatoes with roasted garlic
1/2 c. chicken broth
Garnish: grated Parmesan
   cheese

Heat oil in a skillet over medium heat. Add chicken; sprinkle with
1/2 teaspoon Montreal seasoning. Stir-fry chicken until lightly golden.
Stir in asparagus, mushroom and tomatoes; sprinkle with remaining
Montreal seasoning, parsley, salt and Italian seasoning. Stir and cook
6 minutes. Pour in wine or chicken broth and simmer. Meanwhile,
cook tortellini according to package directions. Add tomatoes with
juice and asparagus mixture. Simmer 7 minutes, slowly add chicken
broth, and continue to simmer 8 minutes. When tortellini is done,
drain and transfer to a large serving bowl. Top with chicken and
asparagus mixture and garnish. Serves 6.

Dijon Chicken & Fresh Herbs

Stacie Avner
Delaware, OH

*I love making this family favorite in the summertime
when my garden is full of fresh herbs!*

4 to 6 boneless, skinless
   chicken breasts
1 t. kosher salt
1 t. pepper

3 to 4 T. Dijon mustard
2 T. fresh rosemary, minced
2 T. fresh thyme, minced
2 T. fresh parsley, minced

Sprinkle chicken with salt and pepper. Grill over medium-high heat
5 to 6 minutes per side, or until juices run clear. Remove from grill
and brush both sides with mustard; sprinkle with herbs. Serves 4 to 6.

Small pleated-paper drinking cups are just the right size
for starting plants. By blowing into the open end, they
will more than double in size. Fill cups with dirt and seeds,
then simply slit the sides of the cups before planting.

Chinese-Style Skirt Steak

Helen Adamson
Winthrop, MA

You really can enjoy your favorite take-out dinner at home...
you won't believe how easy this is to make!

2 lbs. beef skirt or flank steak,
  thinly sliced
1/4 c. oil
1 clove garlic, minced
1 t. salt
1/2 t. pepper
1 t. ground ginger
3 onions, sliced
3 green peppers, sliced
1/4 c. cold water

1/2 c. soy sauce
1 t. sugar
1/2 c. beef broth
1 T. cornstarch
8-oz. can sliced water chestnuts,
  drained
8-oz. can sliced mushrooms,
  drained
cooked rice

In a skillet over medium-high heat, brown beef in oil. Sprinkle in seasonings. Set aside and keep warm. Add onions and peppers to same skillet; cook 3 minutes. Return beef to skillet; stir in remaining ingredients except rice and cook 2 minutes. Spoon over rice to serve. Serves 4 to 6.

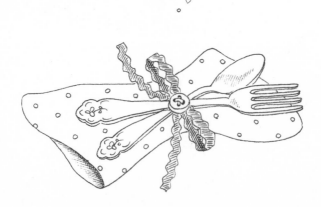

A simple picnic tablecloth made from oilcloth is durable
and easily cleaned...summertime perfect!

Chicken Lo Mein

Jackie Valvardi
Haddon Heights, NJ

Super-simple and tastes terrific!

2 T. soy sauce
2 T. dry sherry or chicken broth
2 t. cornstarch
3/4 lb. boneless, skinless
   chicken breasts or thighs,
   thinly sliced
8-oz. pkg. linguine pasta,
   uncooked
1 T. oil
1 T. toasted sesame oil

8-oz. pkg. sliced mushrooms,
   sliced
1 red or green pepper, cut into
   2-inch strips
4 green onions, cut into 2-inch
   pieces
1-1/2 c. snow pea pods
1/2 c. water
1/4 t. chicken bouillon granules

Whisk together soy sauce, sherry or broth and cornstarch. Add
chicken; stir to coat. Cover and refrigerate 30 minutes. Meanwhile,
cook pasta according to package directions, omitting oil and salt if
called for. Drain well; set aside to keep warm. Add oils to a wok or
skillet over medium-high heat. Stir-fry mushrooms, pepper and onions
in hot oil for 2 minutes. Add pea pods; stir-fry one minute, or until
vegetables are crisp-tender. Remove from skillet and set aside. Drain
chicken, reserving marinade. Stir-fry chicken in same skillet for 2 to
3 minutes, or until no longer pink. Push to sides of skillet. Combine
water, bouillon and reserved marinade; pour into center of skillet.
Bring to a boil; stir constantly, until mixture thickens. Add pasta and
cooked vegetables; stir well to combine. Continue to cook and stir
until ingredients are heated through. Serves 4.

Freeze freshly washed mint
leaves in ice cube trays…
so refreshing in a tall glass
of lemonade or ice water.

Italian Zucchini Casserole

Jeanne Allen
Menomonee, WI

Everyone will ask for seconds of this casserole...
and what a tasty way to eat your veggies!

3 zucchini, sliced
3 T. olive oil, divided
1 onion, sliced
1 clove garlic, minced
28-oz. can diced tomatoes
1 T. fresh basil, minced
1-1/2 t. fresh oregano, minced

1/2 t. garlic salt
1/4 t. pepper
1-1/2 c. favorite-flavor stuffing
  mix
1/2 c. grated Parmesan cheese
3/4 c. shredded mozzarella
  cheese

In a skillet over medium heat, cook zucchini in one tablespoon oil 5 to 6 minutes, or until tender. Drain and set aside. In the same skillet, sauté onion and garlic in remaining oil for one minute. Add tomatoes with juice, basil, oregano, garlic salt and pepper; simmer, uncovered, for 10 minutes. Remove from heat; gently stir in zucchini. Place in an ungreased 13"x9" inch baking dish. Top with stuffing mix; sprinkle with Parmesan cheese. Cover and bake at 350 degrees for 20 minutes. Uncover and sprinkle with mozzarella cheese. Return to the oven and continue baking 10 minutes, or until cheese is bubbly and golden. Makes 6 to 8 servings.

Roasting vegetables is fast & easy. Drizzle sliced veggies
with olive oil, then sprinkle on garlic and onion powder,
salt and pepper to taste. Arrange on a baking sheet
and roast at 350 degrees until crisp-tender.

Cheese & Onion Pie

Jane Kirsch
Weymouth, MA

Originally an English dish, this savory pie is absolutely delicious.

4 c. onion, thinly sliced	3 eggs, beaten
1 T. butter	2/3 c. milk
2 c. favorite shredded cheese	1 t. salt
9-inch deep-dish pie crust	1/4 t. pepper

Sauté onion in butter until tender and golden. Spread alternate layers of onions and cheese in pie crust, ending with cheese. Combine remaining ingredients; beat lightly. Pour over onions and cheese. Bake, uncovered, at 450 degrees for 30 minutes. Makes 4 servings.

Farm-fresh eggs are a delight! This year,
improvise on the traditional Easter basket...
use an upside-down straw hat!

Birdie's Summer Spaghetti

Maryann McGonigle
Greensburg, PA

*I've been called Birdie since I was a very small child.
I like to serve this spaghetti with fresh bread or rolls
and a salad of summertime greens. Very yummy!*

1/4 c. olive oil
2 to 4 cloves garlic, minced
2 tomatoes, diced
1/4 c. fresh basil, sliced
16-oz. pkg. angel hair or penne
  pasta, cooked

3 T. butter
salt and pepper to taste
1/4 c. flat-leaf parsley, chopped
Garnish: grated Parmesan
  cheese

Add oil to a skillet over medium heat. Stir in garlic and cook about
30 seconds. Add tomatoes; stir and sauté until tomatoes become juicy.
Add basil and heat for 3 to 4 minutes. Transfer pasta to a serving
bowl; toss with butter, salt, pepper and parsley. Top with tomato
mixture. Garnish with cheese; toss to coat. Makes 4 servings.

*Be sure to bring the kids along to the farmers' market...
there's so much for them to see! It's good to keep in mind
that for busier, city markets, strollers can be tricky to use
and a baby backpack is a better choice. At a more open,
country market, a wagon will be just right.*

Deb's Garden Bounty Dinner

Deb Grumbine
Greeley, CO

*Great for lunch the next day. Simply shred the chicken
and toss with veggies and rice.*

1 T. oil	1 onion, chopped
4 to 6 chicken legs	2 15-oz. cans stewed tomatoes
6 to 8 zucchini, chopped	2 t. garlic, minced
1 lb. mushrooms, chopped	1 t. turmeric
1 green pepper, chopped	pepper to taste
1 red pepper, chopped	3 c. cooked rice

Heat oil in a skillet over medium-high heat. Add chicken and cook
20 to 25 minutes, or until golden. Set aside and keep warm. Add
remaining ingredients except rice to skillet; cook 5 minutes. Return
chicken to skillet and continue to cook until juices run clear. Serve
alongside servings of rice. Serves 4 to 6.

*Cilantro is easy to grow in full sun and is found in most
Mexican recipes. Let some plants go to seed, and the
gathered seeds are coriander...2 plants in one!*

Honey-Garlic Steak

Athena Colegrove
Big Springs, TX

The honey-garlic sauce is the secret...what a blend of flavors!

1-lb. boneless beef steak
6 T. honey-garlic barbecue
   sauce, divided
2 T. olive oil
1 clove garlic, pressed

1 c. mushrooms, chopped
1 c. green pepper, sliced
1 c. onion, sliced
2 T. soy sauce
cooked rice

Brush each side of steak with one tablespoon barbecue sauce; set aside. Heat oil in a skillet over medium-high heat; stir in remaining ingredients except soy sauce and rice. Sauté 10 minutes, or until vegetables are crisp-tender. Meanwhile, grill steak over medium-low flame for 15 minutes, turning once halfway through cooking time. Add soy sauce and remaining barbecue sauce to vegetables; reduce heat to medium-low. Simmer 15 minutes. Transfer steak to a serving platter, cover with aluminum foil and set aside 5 minutes. To serve, uncover steak, slice and spoon vegetables over top. Serve with rice alongside. Serves 4.

For dinners served at sunset, put a little sand in a simple glass Mason jar and add a tealight. The jar will protect the flickering light from summer breezes. Add a few strings of outdoor twinkle lights to the porch for a soft nighttime glow.

Hawaiian Grilled Chicken

Kristine Coburn
Dansville, NY

If fresh herbs aren't available, simply substitute 1/2 to 3/4 teaspoon dried. This dish is also terrific grilled outside!

1/2 c. olive oil
1/3 c. lemon juice or white wine
   vinegar
1/2 c. soy sauce
3 to 4 cloves garlic, minced
1 to 2 t. fresh oregano, chopped
1 to 2 t. fresh rosemary,
   chopped

4-lb. roasting chicken, halved
Optional: 1 to 2 t. fresh basil,
   chopped
1 t. salt
1/4 t. black or lemon pepper
Garnish: rosemary sprigs, lemon
   wedges

Combine all ingredients except chicken, basil, if using, salt, pepper and garnish in a large plastic zipping bag. Close and shake to blend. Add chicken to bag. Refrigerate up to 6 hours; turn occasionally to coat chicken with marinade. Remove chicken from bag; reserve marinade. Brush chicken with marinade and sprinkle with basil, if desired, salt and pepper. Discard marinade. Place chicken, skin-side down, on a broiler rack about 7 inches from heat. Broil chicken 20 minutes, or until golden. Lightly coat all sides with non-stick olive oil spray. Turn chicken and continue to broil 10 minutes, or until juices run clear. Garnish as desired. Serves 4.

Before serving, brush grilled vegetables with a savory butter blend. Combine 1/4 cup softened butter with 2 tablespoons snipped fresh basil, one clove minced garlic and 1/4 teaspoon pepper.

Pork Mexicali

Becky Hall
Belton, MO

My family really likes this dinner...yours will too!

1 onion, chopped
1 green pepper, chopped
2 stalks celery, chopped
15-oz. can diced tomatoes
15-oz. can black beans, drained
  and rinsed

1/2 t. dried oregano
1/2 t. salt-free seasoning
4 lean pork steaks, about 1-inch
  thick
1 T. oil

Add onion, pepper and celery to a skillet coated with non-stick vegetable spray. Over medium heat, sauté vegetables until crisp-tender. Add remaining ingredients except pork to skillet. Increase heat to medium-high and bring to a boil. Reduce heat and simmer for 5 minutes, stirring often. Transfer mixture to a lightly oiled 1-1/2 quart casserole dish. Brown pork in oil in a skillet over medium-high heat. Arrange over vegetable mixture. Cover and bake at 350 degrees for 20 to 25 minutes, or until pork is tender and cooked through. Serves 4.

Make a soothing chamomile tea bath by filling a cheesecloth bag with chamomile flowers. Tied with jute and hanging from the bathtub faucet, hot water filling the tub will release its sweet fragrance.

A Medley of Sides

Old-Fashioned Creamed Corn

Beverly Tanner
Crouse, NC

This recipe was given to me by my grandmother when I first got married 37 years ago. She has been making her creamed corn this way for 60 years. It always goes first at our church and family suppers, and we always run out...no matter how much I make! This is the best creamed corn you will ever eat!

6 ears corn, husked
1/4 c. bacon drippings
1/4 c. water
2 T. all-purpose flour

1/2 c. milk
sugar to taste
salt and pepper to taste

Remove kernels from corn, reserving as much liquid as possible. Set aside. Heat drippings in a cast-iron skillet over medium heat. Add corn and reserved liquid. Stir in water and cook for 15 minutes. Whisk flour into milk; slowly add to corn. Reduce heat to low and cook, stirring frequently, until mixture thickens. Sprinkle with sugar, salt and pepper; stir to blend. Makes 6 servings.

If you're substituting frozen corn for fresh kernels, a 10-ounce package of frozen equals 1-3/4 cups fresh.

Ann's Veggie Boats

Ann Hole
South Australia, Australia

We all love this dish when we have a barbecue...
my family & friends always ask for seconds!

6 zucchini
1 onion, finely chopped
1 clove garlic, pressed
2 t. butter
1 T. all-purpose flour
1/2 c. milk
1 c. shredded Cheddar cheese

15-oz. can mixed vegetables,
    drained
1 T. fresh dill, chopped
1 T. capers, drained
2 slices bacon, finely chopped
    and crisply cooked
2 T. grated Parmesan cheese

Bring a stockpot of water to a boil over medium-high heat. Add
zucchini and boil for 3 minutes; drain. Slice zucchini lengthwise;
scoop out middles to form boats. In a saucepan over medium heat,
sauté onion and garlic in butter until tender. Stir in flour; continue
cooking for one minute, stirring constantly. Gradually stir in milk.
Continue to stir until sauce boils and thickens. Add Cheddar cheese,
vegetables, dill and capers. Fill zucchini boats with vegetable mixture.
Top with bacon and Parmesan cheese. Arrange on an ungreased
baking sheet and tent loosely with aluminum foil. Bake at
350 degrees until filling is heated through, about 20 to 25 minutes.
Makes 6 servings.

Fresh produce from the market can be made into the tastiest
veggie kabobs. Toss sliced peppers, mushrooms, zucchini, sweet
onion and cherry tomatoes with a drizzle of olive oil. Add
salt and pepper to taste, and thread on metal skewers.
Grill over medium heat, turning after about 5 minutes.

Garlicky Green Beans

Angela DeFrancisco
Millville, NJ

Our family loves garlic and this side dish complements any meal.

3 T. olive oil
2 lbs. green beans, trimmed
1 to 2 cloves garlic, cut into
  slivers

salt and pepper to taste

Heat oil in a saucepan over medium-low heat. Add remaining ingredients; stir and sauté 15 to 20 minutes, to desired tenderness. Serves 6 to 8.

Asparagus with Pecans

Mary Mayall
Dracut, MA

A favorite alongside fish or chicken.

1 bunch asparagus, trimmed
1 t. butter

1/2 c. chopped pecans

Place asparagus in a microwave-safe dish. Microwave, covered, on high setting for 2 minutes. Melt butter in a large saucepan over medium heat. Stir in pecans, stirring constantly, until toasted. Transfer asparagus to saucepan and sauté for 5 to 7 minutes, until tender. Top with pecan mixture. Makes 4 servings.

Try adding toasted garlic and nuts to favorite side dish recipes. Combine chopped nuts with sliced garlic cloves; add to a heavy pan over medium heat. Drizzle with olive oil and toast until golden.

Scrumptious Spinach Pie

Becky Hall
Belton, MO

If you can't make the farmers' market Saturday, don't fret...
a 10-ounce bag of baby spinach from your local grocer
will equal 6 cups fresh spinach.

6 c. baby spinach, trimmed	1 c. milk
1/4 c. onion, chopped	1/3 c. celery, chopped
2 eggs, beaten	1/2 t. salt
2 T. grated Parmesan cheese	1/2 t. nutmeg

Rinse spinach, chop and place in a large saucepan over high heat.
Cook, covered, 5 minutes, or until wilted. Drain, pressing out as much
liquid as possible. Combine remaining ingredients; fold into spinach.
Spoon mixture into a well-greased 9" pie plate. Bake at 375 degrees
for 45 minutes, or until a knife inserted near the middle comes out
clean. Cut into 6 wedges and serve warm. Serves 6.

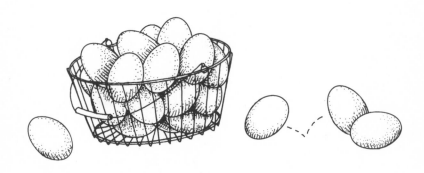

It's easy to tell if the eggs in your refrigerator
are fresh...a fresh egg will sink in water,
a not-so-fresh egg will float.

Golden Squash Patties

Pam Massey
Marshall, AR

This is a summertime favorite at our house!

6 to 8 yellow squash, shredded
1 sweet onion, shredded
salt and pepper to taste
1 c. self-rising flour

1 c. self-rising cornmeal
1 egg, beaten
1 c. shredded Cheddar cheese
oil for frying

Combine squash and onion, sprinkle with salt and pepper and toss to combine. Transfer to a colander and let stand 15 to 20 minutes to allow liquid to drain. Spoon into a large bowl. Alternately add flour and cornmeal, 1/2 cup at a time. Sprinkle again with salt and pepper. Whisk together egg and cheese; stir into squash mixture. Shape mixture into 12 patties. Heat oil in a skillet over medium-high heat. Fry, turning once, until crisp and golden on both sides. Makes one dozen.

It's really personal preference...choose white, yellow
or red onions for anything from salads to cooked dishes.
Sweet onions are best raw, or just very lightly cooked
to keep their sweet, mild flavor.

Crispy Zucchini Fritters

Debra Manley
Bowling Green, OH

So tasty served with ranch dressing for dipping.
I even like to warm the dressing just a bit.

4 zucchini, thickly shredded
1 t. salt, divided
2 eggs, beaten

1/2 t. pepper
1/2 c. all-purpose flour
olive oil for frying

Toss zucchini with 1/2 teaspoon salt. Transfer to a colander and let stand 10 minutes. Drain, pressing out as much liquid as possible. In a large bowl, whisk together eggs, remaining salt and pepper until light and frothy. Whisk in zucchini; stir in flour. Heat oil in a large non-stick skillet over medium-high heat. Drop batter by tablespoonfuls, flattening with the back of spoon. Fry, about 2 minutes on each side, until crisp and golden. Serves 4.

Take your family with you to the market. Kids will
love seeing all there is to enjoy…and a taste of
a warm tomato or juicy peach is a real treat.

3-Cheese Herb Penne

Carol Doggett
Shawnee, KS

One of those classic dishes that pairs perfectly
with a crisp salad and crusty bread...yum!

3 T. butter
2 cloves garlic, minced
1/4 c. all-purpose flour
1 t. dry mustard
1/4 t. nutmeg
3 c. milk
8-oz. pkg. shredded Cheddar
  cheese
1 c. shredded Monterey Jack
  cheese

1/4 c. grated Parmesan cheese
2 T. fresh herbs, finely chopped,
  such as parsley, dill, oregano
  and basil
1/2 t. salt
pepper to taste
16-oz. pkg. penne pasta, cooked

Melt butter in a skillet over medium heat. Add garlic; sauté one
minute. Whisk in flour, mustard and nutmeg. Pour in milk; continue
to whisk until smooth. Bring to a boil, stirring constantly. Reduce heat
and simmer one minute. Combine cheeses; reserve 3/4 cup and set
aside. Add remaining cheese to sauce, a little at a time, stirring until
cheese melts. Add herbs and seasonings. Toss pasta with sauce;
sprinkle with reserved cheese. Spoon into a lightly greased
13"x9" baking pan. Bake, covered, at 350 degrees for 10 to
15 minutes. Uncover and broil for one to 2 minutes, until golden and
bubbly. Serves 4 to 6.

There's no need to cut flowers...a fresh herb bouquet
makes a delightful centerpiece.

Roasted Basil Tomatoes

Denise Neal
Castle Rock, CO

Leftovers are so good served over cooked pasta. Use a potato peeler to get nice slivers of fresh Parmesan cheese.

1/3 c. olive oil
8 to 10 roma tomatoes, halved
   lengthwise
1 to 2 t. dried basil or 1 to 2 T.
   fresh basil, chopped, to taste

salt to taste
Garnish: Parmesan cheese
   slivers

Heat oil in a saucepan over medium heat. Place tomato halves cut-side down in saucepan. Cook 5 to 8 minutes. Arrange tomatoes, cut-side up, in a lightly greased 8"x8" baking pan. Pour any liquid in saucepan over tomatoes. Sprinkle with basil and salt. Bake, uncovered, at 400 degrees for 20 to 30 minutes. Garnish with cheese. Serves 4 to 6.

Stuff a hollowed-out tomato with chicken
or tuna salad for a scrumptious, quick-fix dish.

Herb-Buttered Grilled Corn

Dale Duncan
Waterloo, IA

Try any combination of flavors for the butter. For a tangy flavor,
we love blending butter with just a bit of lime zest and juice.

6 ears corn
1/3 c. butter, softened

2 t. fresh basil, minced
2 t. fresh oregano, minced

Pull back husks of corn, leaving them attached. Remove and discard silk; replace husks around corn. Place corn in a large stockpot; fill with water to cover. Soak 20 minutes; drain. Pull back husks of corn; set aside. Blend butter with herbs and brush evenly over corn; replace husks. Grill corn over medium-high heat, covered, about 15 minutes, until corn is tender. Serves 6.

Oven mitts make it easy to remove the silk from corn.
Just slip the mitts on, then slide your hands over the ears.

Grilled Market Veggies

Regina Wickline
Pebble Beach, CA

*I just love to take my roomy market basket to the farmers' market.
It's great fun to bring home a bushel of veggies, herbs
and new recipes to try!*

2 to 3 zucchini, sliced 3/4-inch thick
2 to 3 yellow squash, sliced 3/4-inch thick
1 to 2 baby eggplant, sliced 3/4-inch thick
1 sweet onion, sliced 3/4-inch thick
2 tomatoes, sliced 1-inch thick

1/2 c. balsamic vinegar
1-1/2 c. oil
2 cloves garlic, minced
1 T. fresh rosemary, minced
1 T. fresh oregano, chopped
1 T. fresh basil, chopped
1 T. fresh parsley, minced
1 T. sugar
salt and pepper to taste

Combine vegetables in a large bowl. Whisk together remaining ingredients and pour over vegetables. Toss to coat. Marinate for 30 minutes to one hour. Remove vegetables from marinade with a slotted spoon. Arrange on a grill over medium-hot heat. Grill 2 to 5 minutes on each side, basting often with marinade, until tender. Makes 4 to 6 servings.

*A salad spinner makes quick work of removing excess
water from freshly washed veggies, fruits and herbs.*

Amy's Garden Pancakes

Amy Wrightsel
Louisville, KY

A savory pancake...perfect alongside grilled chicken or steak.

3/4 c. self-rising white cornmeal
   mix
1/2 c. all-purpose flour
1/2 c. buttermilk
1 egg, beaten
11-oz. can corn, drained
7 green onions, thinly sliced

1/2 red pepper, diced
1 carrot, peeled and shredded
1/2 t. red pepper flakes
1/4 c. oil
Garnish: chopped fresh cilantro,
   sour cream, salsa

Stir together all ingredients except oil and garnish. Heat oil in a skillet over medium-high heat. Drop batter by 1/3 cupfuls into hot oil. Cook 3 to 4 minutes on each side, until golden. Garnish as desired. Makes 10 servings.

Homemade guacamole is a perfect topper spooned on savory pancakes. Make it fresh by blending together 3 pitted, peeled and chopped avocados, 2 cloves pressed garlic, the juice of half a lime and 2 to 4 tablespoons of your favorite salsa.

Grandma Josie's Eggplant

Rosalie Berardo
North Brunswick, NJ

I was lucky to have my Grandma Josie live with us for my whole childhood. I would sit and watch her in the kitchen as much as I could. Having been alive during the Depression, she would never let anything go to waste, so she just threw everything into a pan, and it always tasted good. I am convinced that it was because she "put the love in."

1 eggplant, peeled and cubed
1 egg, beaten
1 onion, finely chopped
2 cloves garlic, minced
1/4 c. grated Parmesan cheese

1-3/4 c. Italian-flavored dry
   bread crumbs, divided
salt and pepper to taste
oil for frying

Bring a stockpot of water to a boil over high heat. Add eggplant and boil until tender. Drain, pressing out as much liquid as possible. Combine eggplant, egg, onion, garlic, cheese, 1/4 cup bread crumbs, salt and pepper. Shape into patties; dip into remaining bread crumbs. Heat oil in a skillet over medium-high heat. Fry patties until golden on both sides. Makes 12 servings.

Making homemade bread crumbs couldn't be easier. Allow bread slices to dry overnight, then pulse them in a food processor. Toss the crumbs with a little butter in a saucepan over medium-low heat and toast until golden.

Market-Fresh Carrots

Jen Licon-Connor
Gooseberry Patch

A zippy side...ready in only 10 minutes!

1 T. olive oil
3 c. baby carrots

1-1/2 T. balsamic vinegar
1 T. brown sugar, packed

Heat oil in a skillet over medium heat. Add carrots; sauté for
10 minutes, or until tender. Stir in vinegar and brown sugar; toss to
coat. Serves 4.

Tangy Summer Slaw

Myra Tunanidis
New Cumberland, WV

This coleslaw is loaded with fresh flavors...it's a must-try!

1 head red cabbage, shredded
1 head green cabbage, shredded
1 carrot, peeled and shredded
1 onion, finely chopped
1 green pepper, finely chopped
16-oz. bottle red wine vinegar &
  oil salad dressing

1/4 c. olive oil
1/4 c. sugar
1 T. Dijon mustard
1 t. caraway seed
salt and pepper to taste

Toss together vegetables in a large serving bowl; set aside. Combine
remaining ingredients; pour over vegetables. Refrigerate until ready to
serve. Toss before serving. Makes 8 to 10 servings.

An edible relish dish! Slice just a bit from the bottom of a
cucumber so it will stand. Then, slice off the top third,
scoop out the seeds and fill with olives and pickles.

Loaded Potato Casserole

Kathy Solka
Ishpeming, MI

The heavenly blend of potatoes, bacon and cheese...
who could ask for more?

20 to 24 new redskin potatoes
seasoning salt, pepper and
   onion powder to taste
1/2 lb. bacon, crisply cooked,
   crumbled and divided

8-oz. pkg. shredded sharp
   Cheddar cheese, divided
1/2 c. butter, melted

Cook potatoes in boiling water until tender; drain. Cool and slice
1/4-inch thick. Arrange half the potatoes in a greased 13"x9" baking
pan. Season as desired and top with half the bacon and half the
cheese. Layer on remaining potatoes; season and top with remaining
bacon and cheese. Drizzle with butter. Bake, uncovered, at
325 degrees until cheese melts and casserole is heated through.
Makes 8 to 10 servings.

Spread savory herb butter over grilled corn or stir it into
whipped potatoes...mmm! To make your own, combine
1/2 pound softened butter with 2 pressed garlic cloves, one
tablespoon each chopped fresh parsley and chives
and 1/2 teaspoon lemon juice.

Savory Cheddar-Onion Pie

Wendy Lee Paffenroth
Pine Island, NY

This is a super serve-along with a ham or beef dinner.

2 c. round buttery crackers,
   crushed
1/2 c. butter, melted
3 to 4 sweet onions, sliced
   1/4-inch
2 T. olive oil

1 c. milk
1/8 t. cayenne pepper
2 eggs, beaten
1 c. shredded Cheddar or
   Monterey Jack cheese

Combine cracker crumbs with butter; set aside one cup. Press remaining crumb mixture into the bottom and up the sides of a 9" deep-dish pie plate. Sauté onions in oil until transparent and tender. Remove with a slotted spoon and spread over crust. In a saucepan over medium heat, combine milk and pepper; without bringing to a boil, cook until heated through. Turn off heat; stir in eggs and cheese. Continue to stir until cheese melts. Spoon over onions; top with reserved crumb mixture. Bake at 325 degrees for 45 minutes. Makes 6 to 8 servings.

Sometimes glass measuring cups get stuck tightly together. Rather than risk breaking the glass, fill the top cup with ice cubes, then place the bottom cup in warm water. The different temperatures will cause them to loosen and be easily pulled apart.

Fried Green Tomatoes

Ginny Schneider
Muenster, TX

Summer squash or okra can also be prepared using this same batter.

1 c. all-purpose flour
1 c. cornmeal
1/2 t. salt

1/2 t. pepper
3 green tomatoes, sliced
oil for frying

Whisk together all ingredients except tomatoes and oil. Dip tomatoes into mixture. Heat oil in a cast-iron skillet; fry tomatoes until golden and crispy on both sides. Makes 4 servings.

Heirloom tomatoes are showing up everywhere. What sets
them apart from more "modern" tomatoes, is that the seeds
have been handed down from one family member to another
for many generations. Give them a try and pick up a
basket the next time you see them!

Kohlrabi Gratin

Katja Meyer-Thuerke
Wattenbek, Germany

In college, my roommate, Anne, and I loved to prepare this recipe served with rice or potatoes. Everyone, even those who had never eaten kohlrabi, loved it. Now, my 2-year-old son, Tjark, thinks it's yummy and can't get enough of it. I love fast recipes like this one...it bakes in only 20 minutes!

1-1/2 lbs. kohlrabi, peeled and
   thinly sliced
1/4 c. oil, divided
2-1/4 c. cooked turkey breast,
   thinly sliced
salt, pepper and nutmeg to taste

2 onions, diced
1 c. whipping cream
1 c. cream cheese with herbs
1/2 c. fresh chives, finely
   chopped
1/2 c. Gruyère cheese, grated

Cook kohlrabi in boiling salted water for 2 to 3 minutes. Rinse with cold water; drain. Heat 2 tablespoons oil in a saucepan over medium-high heat. Cook turkey until golden; add seasonings to taste. Remove from pan and set aside. To the same skillet, add remaining oil and onions. Sauté until golden. Stir in cream and cream cheese. Season again to taste. Reduce heat to medium; stir in chives. Butter a 11"x7" baking pan and layer alternately kohlrabi and turkey in pan. Pour cream sauce over top; sprinkle with Gruyère cheese. Bake, uncovered, at 350 degrees for about 20 minutes. Serves 4.

Fresh herbs...fast!
Use the tines of a
fork to pull leaves from
an herb bundle.

fresh
Herbs

Country Veggie Bake

*Pat Griedl
Appleton, WI*

An easy dinner to toss together, then just pop it in the oven.

1 to 2 T. olive oil
2 carrots, peeled, halved
   lengthwise and sliced
2 onions, chopped
1 to 2 cloves garlic, chopped
1 c. mushrooms, quartered
15-oz. can black beans, drained
   and rinsed
14-oz. can vegetable or chicken
   broth

1 c. frozen corn
1/2 c. pearled barley, uncooked
1/4 c. bulghur wheat, uncooked
1/3 c. fresh parsley, snipped
dried thyme to taste
1/2 to 1 c. shredded Cheddar
   cheese

Heat oil in a large skillet over medium heat. Sauté carrots and onions until carrots are tender. Stir in garlic and mushrooms; sauté 3 minutes. Combine mixture with remaining ingredients except cheese. Spoon into a greased 2-quart casserole dish. Bake, covered, at 350 degrees for one hour, stirring once halfway through baking time. Top with cheese. Cover and let stand 5 minutes, or until cheese melts. Makes 6 servings.

*A side in a snap...cook fresh green beans
with chopped onion and bacon.*

Green Tomato Casserole

Hollie Kouns
Ashland, KY

*This is so good, it's always a hit at get-togethers
and summer cookouts.*

1-1/2 sleeves round buttery
crackers, crushed and divided
3 to 4 green tomatoes, sliced
1/4-inch thick and divided
16-oz. jar mild banana peppers,
drained and divided

8-oz. pkg. shredded Pepper Jack
cheese, divided
2 T. butter, diced

Arrange half the cracker crumbs in a 13"x9" baking pan sprayed with
non-stick vegetable spray. Arrange a layer of green tomato slices on
top of crumbs. Top with half the banana peppers and half the cheese.
Repeat layering again. Top with remaining cracker crumbs and butter.
Bake, covered, at 325 degrees for one hour. Uncover and bake for an
additional 30 minutes. Makes 12 to 15 servings.

*Brussels sprouts make clever placecard holders!
Slice the bottom off each so they sit flat, then cut
a slit in the tops to hold name cards.*

Country Okra Fritters

Martha Fautheree
Midway, TX

This was Grandpa Haston's very favorite dish. During the summer garden harvest, he raised the best okra in the south. The recipe is very simple, using garden-fresh vegetables, but my grandmother had a way of making it so delicious. My grandpa called this "The Haston Special." I am 62 years old now, so this recipe has been passed down for many years in our family.

2 c. okra, sliced
2 to 3 new potatoes, cubed
1 onion, chopped
2 ears corn, kernels removed
1 tomato, chopped
1 green pepper, chopped

salt, pepper and garlic powder
  to taste
1/2 to 2/3 c. all-purpose flour
1/3 to 1/2 c. water
oil for frying

Combine all ingredients except oil together, adding just enough flour and water to hold the ingredients together. Shape into patties. Add 1/4-inch oil to a cast-iron skillet. Fry until golden, 2 to 3 minutes per side. Serves 8 to 10.

Bring a summery bee skep inside for a tabletop centerpiece or set smaller ones across a mantel...fresh and fun!

Apple Orchard Strudel

Cathy Hillier
Salt Lake City, UT

When savory meets sweet, it's a sure-fire winner!

4 c. cabbage, finely chopped
1/4 c. onion, chopped
1-1/2 c. apples, cored, peeled
  and chopped
1/3 c. raisins
1/4 c. sour cream

1 t. mustard
1 c. shredded Cheddar cheese
8 sheets frozen phyllo dough,
  thawed
1/2 c. butter, melted and divided

Add cabbage and onion to a skillet coated with non-stick vegetable spray. Cook, covered, over medium heat for 5 minutes. Combine cabbage mixture with apples and raisins in a large bowl. Stir together sour cream and mustard; add to cabbage mixture. Brush one sheet dough with butter; layer on a second sheet. Continue to brush each sheet of dough with butter and arrange one on top of the other. Spoon cabbage mixture down 1/3 of long side of dough. Top mixture with cheese. Beginning with the long side, roll up jelly-roll style. Place on a 15"x10" jelly-roll pan lightly coated with non-stick vegetable spray. Brush dough with remaining butter. Make 1/4-inch deep cuts about 2 inches apart along the length of the dough. Bake at 400 degrees for 45 minutes. Let stand 5 to 10 minutes before slicing to serve. Serves 6.

A flea-market-find window makes a fun spot to show off sweetly handwritten recipe cards. Place a recipe card in each windowpane with peel & stick photo corners.

Tamara's Pickled Beets

Tamara Ahrens
Sparta, MI

Each year our family attends a summer camp which hosts a terrific salad bar that always serves the best pickled beets. My husband raves about the beets, so I decided to create a recipe to duplicate their wonderful taste.

1/3 c. red wine vinegar
1/3 c. sugar
1/3 c. water
1/2 t. cinnamon
1/4 t. salt

1/4 t. ground cloves
5 whole peppercorns
2 c. beets, peeled, cooked and
   sliced, or 16-oz. can sliced
   beets, drained

Combine all ingredients except beets in a saucepan over medium-high heat. Bring to a boil, stirring constantly. Add beets and return to a boil. Reduce heat and simmer, covered, 5 minutes. Let cool and chill in the liquid for 4 hours to overnight. Store in refrigerator up to 2 weeks. Makes 4 to 6 servings.

Grandma knew how to keep fresh beets
from staining her hands while cutting them...
rub your hands with vegetable oil first!

Aunt Myrtle's Baked Beans

Lucie Wills
Ontario, Canada

My father-in-law prepares these delicious baked beans...
a recipe handed down to him made by his Aunt Myrtle.

1/2 lb. bacon
1 onion, chopped
15-oz. can kidney beans
15-oz. can butter beans
2 20-oz. cans pork & beans

1 c. brown sugar, packed
1/2 c. catsup
2 T. vinegar
1/8 t. garlic powder

In a skillet over medium-high heat, cook bacon and onion together. Drain and reserve drippings. Combine remaining ingredients; stir in bacon, onion and drippings. Spoon into a greased roaster and bake, uncovered, at 350 degrees for 2 hours. Serves 10 to 12.

Sweet little lunchpails bring back the dearest memories.
Tuck a sandwich and some goodies inside to enjoy,
then take a leisurely walk down a country road,
or a welcome nap under the apple tree.

Triple Cheese Mac

Linda Duffy
Mashpee, MA

This is a great dish no matter the season...my family loves it!

6 T. margarine
2 cloves garlic, pressed
1/4 c. all-purpose flour
3-1/2 c. milk
1 T. spicy mustard
salt and pepper to taste
1 c. shredded sharp Cheddar
cheese

1/2 c. shredded American
cheese
1/4 c. grated Parmesan cheese
16-oz. pkg. elbow macaroni,
cooked
1/4 c. bread crumbs

In a saucepan over medium heat, whisk together margarine, garlic
and flour. Stir in milk, mustard, salt and pepper to taste. Cook and stir
until thickened and smooth. Add cheeses, blending well. Stir in
macaroni. Transfer to a greased 13"x9" baking pan. Top with bread
crumbs and bake, uncovered, at 350 degrees until golden, about
35 minutes. Makes 6 servings.

Tie on a cheery calico apron...just because!

Veggie Delight

Michael Curry
Ardmore, OK

*I came up with this recipe because I enjoy broccoli slaw so much.
I added a few more vegetables and tossed on a tangy
Dijon dressing...my family loves it!*

16-oz. pkg. shredded cabbage
1 c. carrots, peeled and grated
1/2 c. broccoli, chopped
1/2 c. cherry tomatoes, halved
1/2 c. celery, sliced
1/2 c. cucumber, peeled and
   diced

1/3 c. olive oil
2 T. vinegar
1 T. Dijon mustard
1 t. garlic salt

Combine vegetables in a large salad bowl. Whisk together remaining
ingredients; drizzle over vegetables. Toss to coat. Makes 10 servings.

*One-pint Mason jars are just right for filling with
crisp salads or layers of fresh fruit and yogurt...
so easy for taking on the road.*

Sassy Squash Blossoms

Lawrie Currin
Dillon, NC

These squash patties are golden and crispy. Yum!

3 c. yellow squash, shredded
2/3 c. biscuit baking mix
1/4 c. butter, melted
1/2 t. salt

1/8 t. pepper
2 eggs, beaten
1/4 c. sweet onion, chopped
oil for frying

Place squash in a colander; press out any liquid. Combine baking mix, butter, salt, pepper and eggs. Stir in squash and onion. Heat about 1/2 inch of oil in a skillet over medium-high heat. Form squash mixture into patties or drop by tablespoonfuls into hot oil. Cook, turning once, until golden on both sides. Remove from skillet and place on paper towels to drain. Makes one to 1-1/2 dozen.

Country-Style Cabbage

Janet Bowlin
Fayetteville, AR

Tossed with bacon and onion, this cabbage side is one tasty way to enjoy your daily dose of veggies!

4 slices bacon, cut into
    1/4-inch pieces
1/4 c. onion, thinly sliced
1 head cabbage, coarsely
    shredded

2 T. sugar
1/4 c. oil, divided
salt and pepper to taste

In a skillet over medium-high heat, cook bacon until crisp. Add onion and cook 2 minutes longer. Stir in cabbage and sugar. Add oil one tablespoon at a time as needed. Cook until cabbage begins to wilt, but is not completely soft. Serve immediately. Makes 4 to 6 servings.

Minted Baby Carrots

Tori Willis
Champaign, IL

Mint is so easy to grow...keep some growing in a sunny spot by the kitchen door, and you can whip up these yummy carrots anytime.

1/2 lb. baby carrots
2 T. butter
salt and pepper to taste

1 T. lemon zest, minced
1 T. brown sugar, packed
2 t. fresh mint, minced

In a stockpot of boiling water, cook carrots 5 minutes. Remove from heat and drain. Melt butter in a skillet over medium-high heat. Stir in carrots; cook until crisp-tender. Season with salt and pepper as desired. Combine remaining ingredients and sprinkle over individual servings. Makes 4 servings.

Farmers' market foods taste so fresh because they're all grown and picked in-season, at the peak of flavor... lettuce, asparagus and strawberries in the springtime, tomatoes, peppers and sweet corn in the summer, squash and greens in the fall and winter.

Orzo with Basil & Prosciutto

Mary Bettuchy
Columbia, SC

If you prefer not to add wine, the step where it's added
and simmered can be omitted...simply skip ahead
to the next step, adding only one cup of broth.

3 shallots, diced
3 cloves garlic, minced
3 T. olive oil, divided
6 thin slices prosciutto, cut into
    1/2-inch pieces
3/4 c. white wine

3/4 c. chicken broth
juice of one lemon
10 fresh basil leaves, chopped
16-oz. pkg. orzo pasta, cooked
1/2 c. shredded Parmigiano-
    Reggiano cheese

In a skillet over medium-high heat, sauté shallots and garlic in
2 tablespoons oil 3 to 4 minutes. Reduce heat to medium; add
prosciutto and sauté one minute. Add wine and reduce heat to low.
Simmer until most of liquid evaporates. Increase heat to medium; add
broth, juice and basil. Stir to combine. Simmer for about 5 minutes.
Add orzo and continue to simmer about 2 minutes, or until most of
the liquid has evaporated. Drizzle with remaining oil and sprinkle with
cheese. Stir to combine. Serves 4 to 6.

Knot the ends of picnic tablecloths then tuck under
to keep them from blowing in the breeze.

Ranch Vegetable Bundles

Patti Walker
Mocksville, NC

I like to make vegetable packets to go along with any main dish I'm serving. They are so easy and I can add meat to them if I want an all-in-one meal. You can also make individual bundles with the vegetables that each family member likes best.

4 potatoes, peeled and sliced
2 zucchini, sliced
2 yellow squash, sliced
8 baby carrots, grated
1 onion, sliced

garlic salt and pepper to taste
1-oz. pkg. ranch salad dressing
  mix
3 T. butter, diced

Place potatoes in the middle of a piece of aluminum foil. Layer zucchini, squash and carrots over potatoes. Add onion; season with garlic salt and pepper to taste. Sprinkle on dressing mix and dot with butter. Fold up ends of aluminum foil over vegetables; secure tightly. Place on a baking sheet and bake at 375 degrees for 30 to 35 minutes. Remove bundles from oven; carefully cut an opening in foil to vent steam before serving. Makes 6 to 8 servings.

Tote market goodies home in true farmgirl style…
tucked inside a roomy wire egg basket!

Summertime Feta & Tomatoes

Rebecca Pickett
Houston, TX

We love to change up the spices and vinegars in this recipe each time we make it. If you eat all the tomatoes and still have dressing left, pour it over your next salad or dip some crusty bread in it!

6 to 7 roma tomatoes, chopped
4-oz. pkg. crumbled feta cheese
1/4 c. olive oil

1/2 c. red wine vinegar
2 t. Italian seasoning
1/4 t. seasoned salt

Combine all ingredients; toss to blend. Refrigerate for 30 minutes to allow flavors to blend. Serves 6 to 8.

Lemony Broccoli

Irene Robinson
Cincinnati, OH

A tang of lemon with fresh broccoli...a winning combination.

1-1/2 lbs. broccoli, cut into
   spears
1/2 clove garlic, minced

2 T. olive oil
2 T. lemon juice

Add broccoli to a saucepan with a small amount of water. Over medium-high heat, cook broccoli 6 to 8 minutes, until crisp-tender. Drain. Sauté garlic in oil over medium heat, until tender. Add lemon juice; mix well. Pour over broccoli, tossing gently to blend. Makes 6 servings.

Check out stores for whimsical polka-dotted snowcone cups...so cute for holding veggies and dip!

Sweet-and-Sour Beans

Ellen Cooper
Mount Vernon, OH

*I tossed this recipe together with what I had on hand
and it's turned out to be a family favorite.*

1 lb. green beans, snapped	1/4 t. pepper
1 onion, sliced	1/4 c. oil
3/4 c. sugar	1/2 t. celery seed
1/2 t. salt	3/4 c. cider vinegar

Combine beans and onion in a serving bowl. Whisk together
remaining ingredients; pour over beans and onion. Refrigerate,
covered, for 3 to 5 hours before serving. Serves 4 to 6.

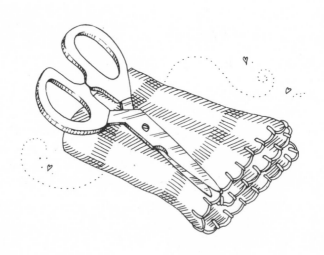

Save time by using kitchen scissors
to trim the ends from fresh green beans.

Sprouting
SALADS

Magnolia Blossom Salad

Francie Stutzman
Dalton, OH

*A simply scrumptious mix of oranges paired with crisp greens
and drizzled with a tangy citrus dressing.*

8 c. mixed salad greens
1/2 c. sweet onion, cut into
   rings
1 avocado, peeled, pitted and
   sliced
2 oranges, peeled and sectioned
2 eggs, hard-boiled, peeled and
   halved lengthwise

2-1/2 t. sugar
1 t. salt
1/4 c. oil
2 T. orange juice
2 T. lemon juice
3 drops hot pepper sauce

Arrange greens in a serving bowl; top with onion. Layer on avocado
and oranges. Remove yolks from eggs; set aside. Dice egg whites and
sprinkle over oranges. Mash egg yolks; blend with remaining
ingredients. Drizzle over salad; toss lightly. Serves 6.

*Snip some blossoms from the farm-fresh bouquet on your
table...there are lots of edible flowers to enjoy. Pesticide-free
blooms like pansies, marigolds, daisies, nasturtium and lilac
are just a few you'll find delicious on fresh salads.*

Sunflower Strawberry Salad

Sister Toni Spencer
Watertown, SD

A great chilled salad...super for hot summer days!

2 c. strawberries, hulled and
   sliced
1 apple, cored and diced
1 c. seedless green grapes,
   halved

1/2 c. celery, thinly sliced
1/4 c. raisins
1/2 c. strawberry yogurt
2 T. sunflower seeds
Optional: lettuce leaves

Combine fruit, celery and raisins. Stir in yogurt. Cover and chill one hour. Sprinkle with sunflower seeds just before serving. Spoon servings over lettuce leaves, if desired. Makes 6 servings.

Tuck several strawberry plants into your garden for a real summertime treat. When you buy plants, you'll find vendors selling two types: June-bearing, which only produce fruit in June, and Ever-bearing, which produce fruit in June, then again in late summer. Whichever you choose, fresh strawberries can't be beat!

Crunchy Green Bean Salad

Fran Jimenez
Granite Bay, CA

Oh, the flavor of this salad…you'll absolutely love it!

1/2 c. honey
1/8 t. cayenne pepper
1-1/2 c. pecan halves
3 T. sherry vinegar
2 t. Dijon mustard
3/4 t. salt
1/2 c. walnut oil

2 lbs. green beans, trimmed
3/4 c. sweetened dried
    cranberries
2 heads Belgian endive,
    trimmed and sliced
    lengthwise
pepper to taste

Stir honey and cayenne pepper together in a saucepan over medium heat until warm. Stir in pecans; pour mixture onto a parchment paper-lined 13"x9" baking pan. Bake at 350 degrees until golden, about 25 minutes, stirring occasionally. Remove from oven and set aside. Whisk together vinegar, mustard and salt. Slowly drizzle in oil, whisking constantly to blend. Fill a large bowl with ice and water; set aside. Add beans to a stockpot, cover with water and bring to a boil. Cook over medium heat until tender, about 2 minutes. Drain and plunge into ice water. Drain, pat dry and place in a large serving bowl. Toss with vinegar mixture to coat. Add nut mixture and remaining ingredients. Toss gently. Serve immediately. Makes 12 servings.

*A weed is only a plant
whose virtues have not yet been discovered.*
-Ralph Waldo Emerson

Icebox Carrot Salad

Susan Hatfield
Pasco, WA

*This is one of my favorite salads. My mother-in-law
shared this recipe with me years ago.*

1/2 c. oil
3/4 c. vinegar
11-oz. can tomato bisque soup
1 c. sugar
1 t. Worcestershire sauce
1 t. pepper

1 t. dry mustard
5 c. carrots, peeled, sliced and
  cooked
1 onion, sliced
1 green pepper, chopped

Combine oil, vinegar, soup, sugar, Worcestershire sauce and spices in a saucepan over medium-high heat. Bring to a boil. Remove from heat and pour over vegetables. Cover and refrigerate overnight. Makes 6 to 8 servings.

Save extra flowers from borage, nasturtium and
Johnny-jump-up plants; rinse and spread the seeds on a
paper towel to dry. Stored in a pretty bottle, they make
a colorful and crunchy topper on your next salad.

Artichoke-Tortellini Salad

Kay Barg
Sandy, UT

*A make-ahead salad that's perfect for toting to a picnic
in the park, girlfriends' lunch or backyard cookout.*

7-oz. pkg. refrigerated cheese
   tortellini
1 c. broccoli flowerets
1/2 c. fresh parsley, finely
   chopped
1 T. pimento, chopped
6-oz. jar marinated artichoke
   hearts

2 green onions, chopped
2-1/2 t. fresh basil, chopped, or
   1/4 t. dried basil
1/2 t. garlic powder
1/2 c. Italian salad dressing
5 to 6 cherry tomatoes, halved
Garnish: sliced black olives,
   grated Parmesan cheese

Cook tortellini according to package instructions. Drain and rinse with
cool water. In a large bowl, combine all ingredients except tomatoes
and garnish. Cover and refrigerate 4 to 6 hours to blend flavors. When
ready to serve, add tomatoes and toss lightly. Garnish with olives and
cheese. Serves 6.

*To choose the best artichokes, look for ones that are dark
green and heavy with tightly closed leaves. If they look dry,
or the leaves are open, the artichokes will be tough.*

Mexican Corn Salad

Kathryn Potter
Chattanooga, TN

I make this recipe for church suppers, family dinners and potlucks at work. Everyone seems to love that it's so versatile. A yummy salad by itself, or add a dollop to grilled salmon or tilapia for a south-of-the-border garnish. Great in summer when fresh sweet corn is plentiful, or prepared with 4 cups thawed frozen corn, it's ready in a jiffy.

8 ears corn, husked
1/4 c. red onion, chopped
1/4 c. green pepper, chopped
1/4 c. red pepper, chopped
1 tomato, chopped
2 t. garlic, chopped
1/4 c. fresh basil, chopped, or
   1 t. dried basil

1 t. dried oregano
Optional: 1 t. hot pepper sauce
1/3 c. olive oil
2 T. lime juice
1 T. rice wine vinegar
salt and pepper to taste
Optional: 1 jalapeño pepper,
   seeded and chopped

Boil corn 8 minutes in a stockpot of lightly salted water. Rinse to cool with cold water; slice kernels from cobs. Combine kernels and vegetables with remaining ingredients except salt, pepper and jalapeño. Toss well to combine. Season with salt and pepper to taste. Add jalapeño, if desired, and toss again. Makes 6 servings

One way to enjoy fresh corn year 'round is to freeze it...and it's so simple! Husk ears and stack them in a large pot, cover with water, bring to a boil and cook for 5 minutes. Remove ears and chill in ice water until they're cool enough to handle. Cut the kernels from the cobs and store in freezer bags.

Poppy Seed Dressing

Marilyn Miller
Fort Washington, PA

A recipe handed down from my mother, it's wonderful drizzled over fresh fruit slices or a fruit salad.

1/2 c. sugar
1 t. salt
1 t. dry mustard
1 t. lemon zest

1 t. onion, grated
1/3 c. lemon juice
3/4 c. olive oil
1 T. poppy seed

Combine all ingredients except poppy seed and mix well. Stir in poppy seed. Refrigerate, covered, until chilled. Makes about 1-1/2 cups.

Log Cabin Salad

Brenda Huey
Geneva, IN

My mom, Iris, lives in a little log cabin by a lake. I named this salad recipe for her.

2 lbs. salad greens
1/2 lb. bacon, crisply cooked
    and crumbled
1 c. chopped pecans
6-oz. pkg. long-grain and wild
    rice, cooked

1 lb. blue cheese, crumbled
2-1/2 c. blueberries, divided
1 to 2 16-oz. bottles poppy seed
    salad dressing

Arrange greens in a large serving bowl. Toss with bacon, pecans, rice, cheese and 1/2 cup blueberries. Mash remaining blueberries and whisk with salad dressing. Drizzle over individual servings. Makes 12 to 15 servings.

For a snappy salad, toss in sliced radishes.
Their peppery flavor is fantastic!

Kim's Specialty Salad

Kim Breuer
Minot, ND

Whenever I bring this to our church picnic there's never any left.

2 heads romaine lettuce, torn
1/2 pt. raspberries
1 avocado, peeled, pitted and
   diced
1 red onion, chopped

3 T. sugar
2-1/4 oz. pkg. sliced almonds
16-oz. bottle poppy seed salad
   dressing

Toss together all ingredients except sugar, almonds and dressing in a large bowl; gently toss. Melt sugar in a saucepan over low heat. Immediately add almonds and toss to coat. Remove almonds from pan and set aside. When cool, break into pieces; add to salad. Gently toss again. Drizzle to taste with dressing. Makes 8 to 10 servings.

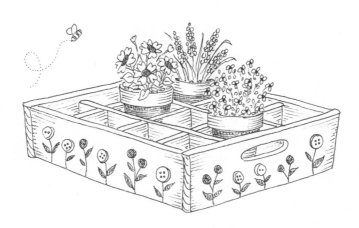

When seedlings are available in the spring, choose some really clever plants for your own garden. Create a garden filled with giant pumpkins, walking-stick cabbages and yard-long runner beans...wait until your friends see these!

Bacony Romaine Salad

Meredith Schaller
Watertown, WI

A tasty salad I love to serve alongside a grilled dinner.

2 heads romaine lettuce,
   chopped
1 sweet onion, thinly sliced

1/2 lb. bacon, chopped
1 c. cider vinegar
1 c. sugar

Arrange lettuce in a large serving bowl. Layer on onion. In a skillet over medium-high heat, cook bacon until crisp; drain. Combine vinegar and sugar; pour into skillet with bacon. Bring to a simmer over medium heat. Cook and stir until sugar dissolves. Pour mixture over lettuce and onion. Toss together and serve immediately. Makes 8 servings.

To make a relaxing herbal pillow, fill a muslin bag with a mixture of rice, dried lavender, crushed cinnamon and whole cloves; stitch closed. To warm the bag, lay it in the microwave for one to 2 minutes on medium-high heat. So nice for soothing sore muscles, or slip it between the sheets for a night of sweet dreams.

Garlic Vinaigrette

Nancy Ramsey
Gooseberry Patch

Add more garlic if you really want the flavor to stand out.

1/3 c. oil
1/3 c. white wine vinegar
2 cloves garlic, minced

1 T. sugar
1/2 t. salt
1/8 t. pepper

Combine all ingredients in a jar with a tight-fitting lid. Secure lid; shake vigorously to blend. Will stay fresh in the refrigerator for up to 2 weeks. Makes 2/3 cup.

Fresh Ranch Dressing

Barbara Voight
Pound, WI

Making your own homemade dressing is easy, and it has such a fresh flavor. We like this dressing spooned over baked potatoes too.

30-oz. jar mayonnaise
1 c. milk
1 T. vinegar
1/2 t. Worcestershire sauce

1 green onion, finely chopped
2/3 c. grated Parmesan cheese
1/2 t. dill weed
1/4 t. pepper

Whisk all ingredients together. Pour into a large jar with a tight-fitting lid. Secure lid and store in refrigerator up to 2 weeks. Makes 1/2 gallon.

Give homemade salad dressings in sweet vintage bottles tied up with a simple herb bouquet.

Turkey Fruit Salad

Beverly Mock
Pensacola, FL

*Host a summertime plant swap with girlfriends, then serve
this delicious salad for lunch. They'll love it!*

3 c. cooked turkey, cubed
3/4 c. celery, chopped
3/4 c. seedless red grapes,
 halved
20-oz. can pineapple chunks,
 drained
11-oz. can mandarin oranges,
 drained

1/4 c. chopped pecans
1/4 c. mayonnaise-type salad
 dressing
1/8 t. salt
Garnish: lettuce leaves

Combine turkey, celery, grapes, pineapple, oranges and pecans
together. Blend in salad dressing; sprinkle with salt. Chill until serving
time. When ready to serve, spoon individual servings onto lettuce
leaves. Serves 4.

*The farmers' market has it all...everything you need
for dinner, a pie for dessert and even flowers for the table!*

Potato Salad for a Crowd

Sherry Rogers
Stillwater, OK

This make-ahead recipe is one that my mother-in-law shared with me.
We always prepare it for family reunions and summertime celebrations.

4 c. mayonnaise-type salad
   dressing
1/4 c. mustard
1 c. sweet pickle relish
1/3 c. white vinegar
1/4 c. sugar
1 T. seafood seasoning
1 t. salt

7 lbs. potatoes, peeled, cubed
   and boiled
8 eggs, hard-boiled, peeled and
   diced
1 yellow onion, finely diced
4-oz. jar diced pimentos,
   drained

Mix together salad dressing, mustard, relish, vinegar, sugar and
seasonings in a very large bowl. Add potatoes; use a potato masher or
pastry blender to mash potatoes. Stir in remaining ingredients. Chill
for one to 2 days before serving. Makes 25 to 30 servings.

Blue, purple, yellow, red and white...potatoes come
in so many colors, try one in a favorite recipe!

Sweet & Tangy Cucumbers

Kathie Poritz
Burlington, WI

I used to work at a deli that served these fantastic
"pickled" cucumbers...this is the secret recipe!

2 c. sugar
1 c. white vinegar
10 to 12 cucumbers, peeled and
    thinly sliced

1 to 2 onions, thinly sliced

Whisk together sugar and vinegar until sugar is dissolved. Toss with
remaining ingredients. Refrigerate until ready to serve. Makes 12 to
15 servings.

Country Market Marinade

Patti Meehleib
Elizabeth, PA

Terrific with any type of veggie...cherry tomatoes, sliced cucumbers,
carrot coins, onions, fresh beans and peas.

3/4 c. canola oil
1/2 c. white vinegar
1 T. salt
1 T. fresh basil, chopped
1 T. fresh tarragon, chopped
1/4 t. pepper

4 tomatoes, sliced
1 cucumber, peeled and thinly
    sliced
1/2 onion, thinly sliced
1 head romaine or iceberg
    lettuce, chopped

Combine all ingredients except vegetables; whisk until well blended.
Combine tomatoes, cucumber and onion; pour marinade over top.
Cover and refrigerate for 5 to 6 hours. Use a slotted spoon to arrange
vegetables over lettuce. Serve with remaining marinade, if desired.
Makes 4 servings.

Patty's Must-Have Salad

*Patty Strock
Liberty Center, OH*

*Whenever I host a family get-together, this salad
is a "must-have" on the menu!*

1 head cauliflower, chopped
2 bunches broccoli, chopped
3 stalks celery, sliced
1 onion, finely chopped
1-1/2 c. shredded Cheddar
   cheese
1 lb. bacon, crisply cooked and
   crumbled

Mix all ingredients in a large bowl. Pour dressing over vegetables; toss until well coated. Makes 18 to 20 servings.

Dressing:

3/4 c. sour cream
1-1/2 c. mayonnaise-type salad
   dressing
1/2 t. lemon juice
1/2 t. salt
1-1/2 t. dill weed
1-1/2 t. sugar

Stir together all ingredients until well blended and smooth.

Re-use and make-do
by dressing up a plain
birdhouse with some
clever finds...a
cast-off spigot
makes a great perch!

Panzanella Salad

Kelly Anderson
Erie, PA

Summer tomatoes are absolutely the best...nothing tastes better than when they're straight from the garden.

2 lbs. heirloom tomatoes, diced
1/4 c. red onion, minced
2 t. garlic, minced
1/2 c. olive oil
2 T. lemon juice
2 T. fresh basil, chopped
1 T. fresh tarragon, chopped

1 t. salt
pepper to taste
Homemade Croutons
2 c. arugula leaves
Garnish: grated Parmesan
   cheese

Place tomatoes in a colander to allow liquid to drain; set aside. Combine remaining ingredients except Homemade Croutons, arugula and garnish. Top with Homemade Croutons and toss well. Divide tomato mixture among 4 serving plates. Top each serving with arugula; garnish with cheese. Serves 4.

Homemade Croutons:

1/4 c. butter
1 T. garlic, minced
6 slices day-old bread, crusts
   trimmed, cubed

salt and pepper to taste
6 T. grated Parmesan cheese

Melt butter in a large skillet over medium heat. Cook until butter foams. Add garlic and cook 30 seconds to one minute. Add bread cubes and toss to coat with butter. Season as desired. Transfer to a baking sheet and bake at 375 degrees for about 15 minutes, or until lightly golden. Sprinkle with cheese and toss until cheese melts. Makes about 6 cups.

Grandma Bev's Greek Salad

Evan Mickley
Delaware, OH

*Whenever Mom makes a salad, my sisters Emma and Gracie and
I always ask... "Is this Grandma Bev's Salad?" It's the best!*

1 c. canola oil
1/3 c. cider vinegar
1-1/2 t. flavor enhancer
1-1/2 t. dried oregano
1-1/2 t. garlic powder
1-1/2 t. salt

1 head romaine lettuce, torn
1/2 cucumber, cubed
1/2 c. grape tomatoes, halved
1/4 red onion, thinly sliced
Optional: crumbled feta cheese
Garnish: croutons

Combine oil, vinegar and seasonings in a jar with a tight-fitting lid;
shake until thoroughly blended. Set aside. Add remaining ingredients
except croutons to a large salad bowl. Toss with dressing to taste;
garnish with croutons. Makes 4 to 6 servings.

*While poppy seed dressing is delicious on your
favorite salad, it's also yummy drizzled
over slices of fresh fruit!*

Laurel's Fruit Salad

Laurel Perry
Loganville, GA

Anytime I make this for a church social or potluck,
I get requests for the recipe. It's so light and refreshing.

1 pineapple, cored, peeled and
    sliced
1 qt. strawberries, hulled and
    sliced
1/2 c. blueberries
1/2 c. raspberries
2 c. Red Delicious apples, cored
    and chopped

4 oranges, peeled and sectioned
2 bananas, sliced
2 c. orange juice
1 c. sugar
1 t. almond extract
1 t. vanilla extract

Combine fruit in a large bowl. Combine remaining ingredients, stirring until sugar dissolves. Pour over fruit mixture, tossing lightly. Chill 2 to 3 hours before serving. Makes 12 servings.

Plan a summer afternoon of crafty fun. Felted wool makes
the sweetest flower pins, pincushions and mug mats.
Friends can bring supplies to share... you set out
some yummy food and beverages.

Blueberry-Chicken Salad

Debi DeVore
Dover, OH

Fresh blueberries and lemony yogurt add a fresh spin
to the "usual" chicken salad.

2 c. chicken breast, cooked and
  cubed
3/4 c. celery, chopped
1/2 c. red pepper, diced
1/2 c. green onions, thinly sliced

2 c. blueberries, divided
6-oz. container lemon yogurt
3 T. mayonnaise
1/2 t. salt
Optional: Bibb lettuce

Combine chicken and vegetables in a large bowl. Gently stir in 1-1/2 cups blueberries; reserve remaining berries. Blend remaining ingredients except lettuce. Drizzle over chicken mixture and gently toss to coat. Cover and refrigerate 30 minutes. Spoon onto lettuce-lined plates, if desired. Top with reserved blueberries. Makes 4 servings.

Bring back a bit of old-fashioned neighboring...
chat across the backyard fence, deliver a warm pie,
share a bouquet of sunflowers.

Quick & Easy Veggie Salad

Dana Thompson
Gooseberry Patch

*A trip to the town market and I have all I need
for this quick & easy salad.*

1/2 head cauliflower, chopped
1 bunch broccoli, chopped
1 tomato, chopped

1/4 red onion, sliced
3 to 4 T. Italian salad dressing

Combine cauliflower, broccoli, tomato and onion in a serving bowl. Toss with dressing to taste. Serves 4.

Whether it's an afternoon with friends or a family reunion, set up a summery get-together in farmgirl style using wooden ironing boards as serving tables. Tack a clothesline around the ironing board edge, and use clothespins to secure sweet vintage hankies or dandy aprons in place.

Kathleen's BLT Salad

Kathleen Harden
Latrobe, PA

I used to make stuffed tomatoes but they always seemed so time-consuming so I came up with this salad version. It's also a wonderful, tasty way to use up those healthy, fresh tomatoes from the garden!

1 to 2 T. mayonnaise
1 t. vinegar
1/8 t. seafood seasoning
1/4 head iceberg lettuce, torn
   into bite-size pieces

2 tomatoes, cut into wedges
1/2 c. bacon, crisply cooked and
   crumbled
1/2 c. shredded Cheddar cheese

Whisk together mayonnaise, vinegar and seasoning. Set aside. Arrange lettuce and tomatoes on salad plates. Top with bacon and cheese. Drizzle with dressing. Toss before serving. Makes 2 servings.

One of the best things about the farmers' market…everything is locally grown, in season. Plump strawberries are ready in June; blueberries and beans in July; corn, melons and peaches in August; and apples and pumpkins in October.

Chinese Coleslaw

Carolyn Ayers
Kent, WA

Crunchy, colorful and full of flavor, but it's the dressing
that really makes this a stand-out!

9 c. Napa cabbage, shredded
4 c. green cabbage, shredded
1 c. red or green pepper, sliced
1 c. snow pea pods

1 c. bean sprouts
5 green onions, sliced
Garnish: 2 T. toasted sesame
   seed

Combine vegetables in a large bowl. Drizzle with Sesame-Ginger
Dressing; toss and sprinkle with sesame seed. Toss once more before
serving. Makes 12 servings.

Sesame-Ginger Dressing:

1 clove garlic, minced
1/8-inch thick slice fresh ginger,
   peeled and minced
1/4 c. sesame seed oil or peanut
   oil

3 T. soy sauce
3 T. rice wine vinegar
1 t. sugar
Optional: 4 drops chili oil

Combine all ingredients in a jar with a tight-fitting lid. Secure lid and
shake well to blend.

Why not set up a stand on the town square with other vendors?
There's so much you can share...homegrown veggies, fruit,
homebaked pies and bread, plant starts, herbs or flowers.
Set up your table and smile!

Celebration Salad

Lori Costello
Dubuque, IA

This recipe is a great spring and summer salad, and is always requested for get-togethers. It has a nice sweet cucumber taste to it.

16-oz. pkg. spiral pasta, uncooked
1/2 c. celery, chopped
1/2 c. onion, chopped
2 c. carrots, peeled and shredded
1 c. green or red pepper, shredded
1 c. cucumber, chopped
1 c. vinegar
1-1/2 c. sugar
14-oz. can sweetened condensed milk
2 c. mayonnaise-type salad dressing

Cook pasta according to package directions. Drain and rinse with cold water; drain again. Toss pasta and vegetables together in a serving bowl. Whisk remaining ingredients together until well blended and sugar is dissolved. Drizzle over vegetables; toss to coat. Refrigerate overnight. Makes 15 to 20 servings.

Celebrate special occasions with a cheery banner hanging along the front porch or over the fireplace. They're easy to make using pretty papers, pinking shears and ribbon. Cut out paper letters, punch holes for hanging and string on ribbon.

Apple-Yogurt Coleslaw

Lane McCloud
Siloam Springs, AR

The tart flavor of the apples, sweetness of the pineapple and cranberries and the crunch of the nuts add a fresh twist to coleslaw.

1 c. plain or vanilla yogurt
1/4 c. mayonnaise
8-oz. can crushed pineapple
4 Granny Smith apples, cored
   and chopped
1/2 head purple cabbage,
   shredded
1/2 head green cabbage,
   shredded
1/4 c. red onion, finely chopped

1 carrot, peeled and shredded
1 stalk celery, diced
1/4 c. sugar
1/2 t. salt
1/4 t. pepper
1 t. mustard
3/4 c. sweetened dried
   cranberries
3/4 c. chopped walnuts
Garnish: cabbage leaves

Mix together yogurt, mayonnaise and pineapple with juice in a large bowl. Stir apples into yogurt mixture, coating well. Add remaining ingredients except cranberries, walnuts and garnish; mix well. Cover and chill for at least one hour. Before serving, stir in cranberries and walnuts. Serve on whole cabbage leaves. Makes 8 to 10 servings.

Recycle with style! Label colorful
metal buckets with stick-on vinyl letters.

Dijon-Honey Vinaigrette

Cindy Neel
Gooseberry Patch

Wonderful on fresh salads or steamed veggies.

1 c. oil
1/2 c. white vinegar
1 T. honey
1 T. Dijon mustard

1/2 t. pepper
2 t. salt
2 t. garlic, minced
4 drops hot pepper sauce

In a small bowl, whisk together all ingredients until thoroughly combined. Pour into a jar; secure lid and chill until ready to serve. Makes about 1-1/2 cups.

Very Berry Vinaigrette

Angela Murphy
Tempe, AZ

A can't-miss dressing...yummy on spinach salad.

1/4 c. olive oil
1 c. seasoned rice vinegar

10-oz. jar seedless raspberry jam

Combine all ingredients in a blender; blend until smooth. Refrigerate, covered, until ready to serve. Makes about 2-1/2 cups.

Fill vintage bottles with homemade vinaigrette to share with girlfriends...they'll be tickled!

Tomato-Garbanzo Salad

Aubrey Dufour
Salem, IN

*Try this salad the next time you're looking for
something new to tote to a get-together.*

7-oz. pkg. elbow macaroni,
  uncooked
15-oz. can garbanzo beans,
  rinsed and drained
2 c. tomatoes, diced
1 c. celery, diced
1/2 c. red onion, diced

1/3 c. olive oil
1/4 c. lemon juice
2 T. fresh parsley, chopped
2 t. ground cumin
2 t. salt
1/2 t. pepper

Remove one cup macaroni from package; save remaining macaroni
for use in another recipe. Cook macaroni according to package
directions; drain. Rinse in cold water; drain again. Transfer to a large
bowl and combine with remaining ingredients. Stir to mix well. Cover
and chill at least one hour. Makes 6 servings.

Serve baskets of crackers or rolls to go with salads on a
dressed-up enamelware tray. Cut a fun and flowery fabric
to fit the edges of the tray. Coat the tray surface with a
spray adhesive, center the fabric, smoothing out
completely, then set aside to dry.

FRESH
Soups
& Bountiful
Breads

Iowa's Best Corn Soup

Kay Marone
Des Moines, IA

Iowa is corn country, and this soup is a local favorite.

1 t. olive oil
1/2 c. onion, diced
1 clove garlic, minced
1/2 t. ground cumin
4 c. fresh corn kernels
2 new potatoes, diced

1/2 t. kosher salt
1/8 t. pepper
4 c. vegetable broth
3/4 c. milk
1 t. fresh cilantro, chopped

Heat oil in a stockpot over medium heat. Sauté onion, garlic and cumin for 5 minutes, or until onion is tender. Add remaining ingredients except milk and cilantro; bring to a boil. Reduce to a simmer and cook for 20 minutes, or until potatoes are tender. Add milk and cilantro; cook and stir to heat through. Makes 8 servings.

The difference between really sweet, tender corn and tough corn is all in when it's picked. Ideally you want to pick it, cook it and enjoy it the same day.

Creamy Asparagus Soup

Elaine Slabinski
Monroe Township, NJ

Asparagus is very plentiful in our garden in the spring and this is a family favorite...it tastes even better the next day.

1 to 1-1/2 lbs. asparagus,
   trimmed and chopped
14-1/2 oz. can chicken broth
1 T. onion, minced

1 t. salt
1/4 t. white pepper
1/2 to 3/4 c. half-and-half

Set aside asparagus tips for garnish. Combine remaining ingredients except half-and-half in a soup pot over medium heat. Bring to a boil; reduce heat and simmer 5 to 7 minutes, or until asparagus is tender. Working in small batches, ladle asparagus mixture into a blender. Add half-and-half to taste and purée. Return mixture to soup pot and heat through without boiling. Steam or microwave reserved asparagus tips just until tender; use to garnish soup. Makes 4 servings.

MOO!

If you're out of half-and-half for a savory, summertime soup, substitute 4-1/2 teaspoons melted butter plus enough milk to equal one cup. You can also use an equal amount of evaporated milk.

7-Veggie Slow-Cooker Stew

*Eileen Miller
Cleveland, OH*

*The slow cooker does all the work, while you catch up
on the latest gardening magazine.*

1 butternut squash, peeled,
    seeded and cubed
2 c. eggplant, peeled and cubed
2 c. zucchini, diced
10-oz. pkg. frozen okra, thawed
8-oz. can tomato sauce
1 c. onion, chopped
1 tomato, chopped
1 carrot, peeled and thinly sliced

1/2 c. vegetable broth
1/3 c. raisins
1 clove garlic, chopped
1/2 t. ground cumin
1/2 t. turmeric
1/4 t. red pepper flakes
1/4 t. cinnamon
1/4 t. paprika

Combine all ingredients in a slow cooker. Cover and cook on low
setting for 8 to 10 hours, or until vegetables are tender. Serves 10.

Fresh herbs will taste their best stored for just a few days in
an open or perforated plastic bag in the refrigerator. If you
want to keep them more than a few days, snip off the ends
and arrange them in a tall glass with an inch of water.
Covered loosely with a plastic bag, they'll last a week or more.

Great-Aunt Clarissa's Soup

Debbie Gillam
Tipton, IN

This recipe is from my Great-Aunt Clarissa, who, at over 90 years of age, is still an avid gardener. If you'd like, combine the ingredients in a slow cooker, cover and cook on low setting for 4 to 6 hours.

2 to 3 yellow squash, cut into
   1/2-inch cubes
2 to 3 zucchini, cut into
   1/2-inch cubes
2 14-1/2 oz. cans diced
   tomatoes

1 onion, chopped
2 to 3 cloves garlic, minced
1 lb. smoked turkey sausage,
   cut into bite-size pieces

Combine all ingredients in a soup pot and bring to a boil. Reduce heat and simmer, stirring occasionally, for one to 2 hours, or until vegetables are tender. Makes 4 servings.

Put your soup supper together the night before.
Peel and chop vegetables and store in plastic zipping
bags in the refrigerator. In the morning, simply
add all soup ingredients to the slow cooker.

Aunt B's Sweet Butter Bread

Bryna Dunlap
Muskogee, OK

There's just nothing like the aroma of bread while it's baking. This is my own recipe...it's nice to bake one loaf to keep and one to share.

2 t. active dry yeast
1-1/8 c. warm water
2 c. all-purpose flour
2 c. whole-wheat flour
2 T. powdered milk

1/4 c. honey
2 t. salt
1/4 c. butter, softened
1 egg, beaten
1/4 c. butter, melted

Dissolve yeast in warm water, between 110 and 115 degrees. Combine remaining ingredients, except melted butter, in a bowl. Add yeast mixture; stir to blend. Turn dough out onto a lightly floured surface; knead until smooth. Cover with a cloth and let rise until double in size. Form into 2 loaves and place each in a lightly oiled 9"x5" loaf pan. Place loaves in a cold oven and set temperature to 325 degrees. Bake for 20 minutes, or until golden. Remove from oven and brush tops with melted butter. Makes 2 loaves.

Summer Herb Butter

Vickie

A pot of herbs growing in a sunny spot by the back door is so nice... just snip fresh herbs whenever you need them!

1/2 c. butter, softened
1/4 c. fresh herbs, chopped,
    such as basil, thyme, sage,
    parsley, dill, chives, tarragon,
    oregano, marjoram or
    rosemary

1 t. sea salt
1 t. pepper

Blend all ingredients together. Spoon onto a sheet of wax paper and shape into a log. Twist ends of wax paper to seal. Refrigerate one hour to allow flavors to blend. Use within 2 weeks. Makes 1/2 cup.

Country Minestrone Soup

Erica Clopton
Fort Worth, TX

This tasty recipe was given to me by my mother-in-law.

3 slices bacon, diced
1 c. onion, chopped
1/2 c. celery, sliced
14-1/2 oz. can beef broth
10-3/4 oz. can bean with bacon
    soup
1-3/4 to 2 c. water
1 t. dried basil
1/2 t. salt

1/2 t. pepper
14-1/2 oz. can diced tomatoes
8-oz. pkg. elbow macaroni,
    uncooked
1 c. cabbage, chopped
1 c. zucchini, cubed
1 c. yellow squash, cubed
1/2 t. beef bouillon granules

In a skillet over medium-high heat, cook bacon until crisp. Use a
slotted spoon to remove bacon and set aside to drain, reserving
drippings. In the same skillet, sauté onion and celery in drippings until
tender. Stir in broth, soup, water, basil, salt, pepper and tomatoes.
Bring to a boil; reduce heat and simmer 10 minutes. Add remaining
ingredients except reserved bacon. Simmer for 10 minutes, or until
macaroni and vegetables are tender. Stir in bacon. Serves 6 to 8.

Backpacks are ideal for visits to the farmers' market.
They keep your hands free to shop, and are perfect
for tucking keys, money and other necessities into.

Garlicky Tomato Soup

Diana Chaney
Olathe, KS

Summertime tomatoes are my absolute favorite vegetable...
nothing even compares to them! This soup is especially tasty
served with homemade bread brushed with melted herb butter.

3 tomatoes, cubed
2 green, red or yellow peppers,
   cut into bite-size pieces
10 cloves garlic, coarsely
   chopped and divided

1/2 c. olive oil
2 c. water
2 t. salt
pepper to taste

Combine tomatoes, peppers and half the garlic in a food processor.
Pulse until tomatoes and peppers are chopped; set aside. Heat oil in a
saucepan over medium heat. Add tomato mixture and cook, stirring
often, about 5 minutes. Add remaining ingredients; bring to a boil.
Reduce heat to low and simmer for 10 minutes. Serves 4.

Add cubes of toasted sourdough or herb bread
to the bottoms of soup bowls and ladle
in steaming soup. Yummy!

Cheddar Cheese & Chive Soup

Gladys Kielar
Perrysburg, OH

Fresh garlic and chives give this cheesy soup an amazing taste.

14-1/2 oz. can vegetable broth
1 t. dried, minced onion
1/2 t. garlic, minced
1 T. fresh chives, chopped

8-oz. pkg. shredded Cheddar
  cheese
1/2 c. milk

Mix all ingredients except cheese and milk in a soup pot. Bring to a boil over medium heat. Add cheese; stir to melt. Reduce heat to low; stir in milk. Simmer until heated through. Makes 4 servings.

Here's a super-quick recipe for making your own veggie wash. Combine one tablespoon lemon juice, 2 tablespoons baking soda, one cup water and 3/4 cup white vinegar in a spray bottle. Shake well to blend, spray fresh produce and let sit 5 minutes. Rinse well before using.

Summer Squash Chowder

Cheryl Donnelly
Arvada, CO

I love this soup in the late summer and early fall when the garden and farmers' markets are bursting with fresh produce. If it's made off-season, frozen corn is a good substitute...just reduce the cooking time to 2 minutes once it's added.

4 slices bacon, chopped
1 onion, finely diced
1 clove garlic, minced
1 yellow or red pepper, finely
   diced
2 T. all-purpose flour
14-1/2 oz. can vegetable broth,
   divided
5-oz. can evaporated milk
4 zucchini, diced
2 yellow squash, diced

1 t. white wine Worcestershire
   sauce
1/2 t. hot pepper sauce
3/4 t. dried thyme
1/2 t. salt
1 c. fresh corn kernels
2 T. lemon juice
1/2 c. fresh parsley, finely
   chopped
pepper to taste

In a soup pot over medium heat, cook bacon until crisp. Set aside bacon and drain, reserving drippings in soup pot. Add onion, garlic and yellow or red pepper into soup pot; sauté 5 minutes. Sprinkle flour evenly over vegetables and cook one minute. Add 1/2 cup broth, stirring well to blend. Cook over medium heat until thickened. Pour in remaining broth, milk, zucchini, squash, sauces, thyme and salt. Bring to a boil. Reduce heat and simmer, covered, 15 minutes, stirring occasionally. Add corn to a saucepan; cover with water. Cook over medium heat 5 minutes. Drain and stir into soup mixture. Add reserved bacon, juice and parsley. Heat through and add pepper to taste. Makes 4 servings.

What man needs in gardening,
is a cast-iron back with a hinge on it.
-Charles Dudley Warner

Oniony Zucchini Soup

Kristine Coburn
Dansville, NY

A great and different way to enjoy your summer bounty!

3 T. butter
1 T. olive oil
3 yellow onions, halved and
   sliced
2 cloves garlic, minced
3 lbs. zucchini, sliced

1 c. white wine or chicken broth
salt and pepper to taste
3 c. chicken or vegetable broth
1/2 c. whipping cream
1/4 t. nutmeg

Heat butter and oil over medium heat in a large stockpot. Add onions and cook until tender. Stir in garlic and zucchini; cook 5 minutes. Add wine or chicken broth; stir in salt and pepper. Cook until liquid is reduced by half; add chicken or vegetable broth. Bring to a boil and cook until zucchini is tender. In a blender, purée soup to desired consistency. Stir in whipping cream and nutmeg. Garnish with Parmesan Croutons. Serves 8.

Parmesan Croutons:

1-1/2 c. day-old French bread,
   diced
1/4 c. olive oil
2 T. fresh oregano, finely
   chopped

1/4 c. grated Parmesan cheese
salt to taste

Toss bread with oil. Arrange on an ungreased baking sheet and bake at 375 degrees until lightly golden. Toss with remaining ingredients to coat.

For the price of a stamp, you can put some flower or veggie seeds in an envelope to swap with friends. It's such fun to see what they send back to you!

Herb Focaccia Bread

Irene Robinson
Cincinnati, OH

*This crispy, crunchy bread is easy to make
and bakes in only 10 minutes.*

11-oz. tube refrigerated French
   bread dough
2 T. olive oil
1 t. kosher salt
1 t. pepper

1 t. dried oregano
1 t. dried basil
1/2 t. dried thyme
Optional: marinara sauce,
   warmed

Unroll dough and pat into an ungreased 15"x10" jelly-roll pan. Press
the handle of a wooden spoon into dough, making indentations
one inch apart. Drizzle with oil and sprinkle with remaining
ingredients except sauce. Bake at 375 degrees for 10 minutes, or until
golden. Cut in rectangles and, if desired, serve with warm marinara
sauce for dipping. Serves 8.

Kosher salt has big crystals and a distinct flavor from ordinary
table salt. Try it in your next recipe…just remember that one
tablespoon of kosher salt is equal to 2 teaspoons of table salt.

Tomato & Corn Chowder

Sandy Roy
Crestwood, KY

The flavor of this chowder is so exceptional
that I've been making it for almost 30 years.

3 T. butter
1 onion, chopped
1 clove garlic, minced
1/2 c. celery, thinly sliced
1 c. carrot, peeled and shredded
4 ears corn, kernels removed
2 potatoes, peeled and diced
3 tomatoes, peeled and coarsely
   chopped

1 t. sugar
1 t. salt
1/2 t. white pepper
1/4 c. fresh basil, chopped
3 c. water
1 T. vegetable bouillon granules
1 c. half-and-half
Garnish: chopped fresh parsley
   or thinly sliced green onions

In a large stockpot over medium heat, combine butter, onion, garlic, celery and carrot. Cook for 20 minutes, or until vegetables are tender. Add remaining ingredients except half-and-half and garnish. Reduce heat and simmer, stirring occasionally, 35 to 40 minutes, or until vegetables are tender. Stir in half-and-half and garnish as desired. Makes 6 to 8 servings.

Top servings of soups and salads with homemade croutons... they're so simple to make. Melt 1/4 cup butter in a skillet over medium heat. Stir in 3 cups of bread cubes and toss to coat. Cook, stirring occasionally, until golden and crisp. Sprinkle with salt or pepper, if desired.

Chilled Melon Soup

Janice Woods
Northern Cambria, PA

*This delicious and beautiful recipe is perfect for summer
get-togethers with friends.*

3 c. cantaloupe melon, peeled,
   seeded and chopped
2 T. sugar, divided
1/4 c. orange juice, divided
1/8 t. salt, divided

3 c. honeydew melon, peeled,
   seeded and chopped
Garnish: fresh mint sprigs or
   orange slices

In a blender, process cantaloupe, half the sugar, half the juice and half
the salt until smooth. Cover and refrigerate. Repeat with honeydew
and remaining ingredients except garnish. Refrigerate, covered, in
separate containers. To serve, pour equal amounts of each mixture at
the same time on opposite sides of individual soup bowls. Garnish as
desired. Makes 4 to 6 servings.

*Here's a handy way to easily pour two flavors of chilled soup
into a bowl at the same time. Fill two small cream pitchers
with each flavor of soup, then pour. The pitchers'
small size makes pouring so easy!*

Strawberry-Peach Soup

Kathy Majeske
Denver, PA

This is great on hot summer days or for a ladies' luncheon.
Not only does it taste great...it looks great!

2 c. strawberries, hulled and
  chopped
8-oz. container strawberry
  yogurt
1/2 c. sugar, divided
1 t. lemon juice, divided

2 peaches, pitted, peeled and
  chopped
8-oz. container peach yogurt
Garnish: whipped cream,
  strawberries

Combine strawberries, strawberry yogurt, 1/4 cup sugar and
1/2 teaspoon lemon juice in a blender. Process until smooth. Transfer
to a bowl and set aside. Repeat with remaining ingredients except
garnish. To serve, pour each mixture at the same time into individual
shallow soup bowls. Garnish servings with whipped cream and a
strawberry. Makes 6 servings.

Nectarines can be used in the same recipes as peaches.
The only difference between the two is the lack of fuzz
on the nectarine and they tend to be a bit smaller in size.

Crystal's Vegetable-Beef Soup

Crystal Willich
Horton, KS

*I created this recipe when I couldn't find a similar slow-cooker recipe
using cabbage. I like to use both the slow cooker and stovetop...
I just think it has a better taste this way!*

1-1/2 lb. beef chuck roast
3 14-1/2 oz. cans beef broth
2 1-oz. pkgs. onion soup mix
1 to 2 c. baby carrots

10-oz. pkg. frozen peas, thawed
1 head cabbage, finely chopped
8-2/3 c. cocktail vegetable juice

Combine beef, broth and soup mix in a slow cooker. Cover and cook
on low setting for 8 hours. Stir in carrots and cook until almost tender.
Transfer meat and carrots from slow cooker to a soup pot. Add
remaining ingredients; stir and cook approximately one hour, or until
carrots and cabbage are tender. Serves 8.

*Look for the bright colors and fun graphics on old soda
crates...they make clever and stylish veggie bins!*

Garden-Fresh Gazpacho

Patsy Johnson
Salem, MO

I learned to make this when I was managing a restaurant.
It can be very addictive in the summer months!

6 to 8 tomatoes, chopped
1 onion, finely chopped
1 cucumber, peeled and chopped
1 green pepper, chopped
2 T. fresh parsley or cilantro,
  chopped
1 clove garlic, finely chopped

1 to 2 stalks celery, chopped
2 T. lemon juice
salt and pepper to taste
4 c. tomato juice
4 drops hot pepper sauce
Optional: sour cream

Combine all ingredients except sour cream, if using, in a large lidded container or gallon-size Mason jar. Refrigerate until well chilled. Dollop servings with sour cream, if desired. Serves 12 to 15.

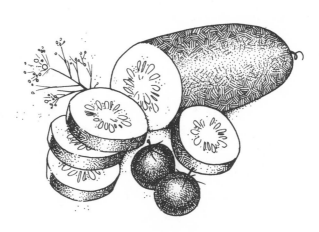

In any favorite gazpacho recipe, swap out the
tomatoes for avocados, or try unflavored yogurt
for a yummy white gazpacho.

Caroline's Leek Soup

Laura Fuller
Fort Wayne, IN

*After many trips to the farmers' market, I began chatting with Caroline.
She always has the same corner spot that's bursting with herbs and
fresh produce. One Saturday she shared this recipe with me, and our
family's been enjoying it ever since.*

1 leek, halved lengthwise and sliced	3/4 t. coriander
1 t. butter	14-1/2 oz. can chicken broth
1 T. water	1-1/4 c. milk
1 head cauliflower, cut into 1-inch pieces	1-1/4 t. salt
	1/4 t. pepper
	Garnish: 1 T. sliced almonds

Rinse leek well in cold water; pat dry. In a saucepan over medium-
high heat, combine butter and water. Add leek and cauliflower; cook
for 5 minutes. Stir in remaining ingredients except garnish and bring
to a boil. Reduce heat to low and simmer, covered, 20 minutes.
Transfer soup in batches to a blender; purée until smooth. Garnish
servings with almonds. Serves 4.

*To quickly clean leeks, slice them into 2-inch lengths and soak
in a bowl of cold water. Swish them in the water and drain.
Refill the bowl, and swish again until the water is clear.
They're ready to use…simply drain and pat dry.*

Patchwork Soup

Nola Coons
Gooseberry Patch

This savory soup cooks in under 20 minutes.

2 T. butter
2 c. leeks, chopped
1/4 c. shallots, minced
3 cloves garlic, chopped
6 T. fresh Italian parsley, finely chopped and divided
2 T. fresh thyme, chopped
1 T. fresh oregano, chopped

1 red pepper, cut into 1/4-inch cubes
8 c. chicken broth
10-oz. pkg. frozen baby lima beans
10-oz. pkg. frozen shoepeg corn kernels
14-3/4 oz. can creamed corn

Melt butter in a large heavy saucepan over medium heat. Stir in leeks, shallots and garlic; sauté until leeks are tender. Add 4 tablespoons parsley and remaining herbs. Cook for 2 to 3 minutes. Stir in pepper, broth and beans; bring to a boil. Reduce heat to low and simmer 10 minutes, or until beans are tender. Stir in remaining ingredients and heat through. Garnish servings with remaining parsley. Makes 10 servings.

Dress up plain tea towels by adding mini flour sack squares with a hand-embroidery stitch. They're so sweet wrapped around mini loaves of bread or rolls...a gift anyone will love.

Garlicky Bubble Bread

Annette Ingram
Grand Rapids, MI

I first saw bubble bread in a little bakery on the town square and decided to try my hand at making my own. This version is so simple, we can enjoy it anytime.

2 eggs, beaten
3 T. green onions, finely
   chopped
3 T. fresh parsley, chopped
1-1/2 t. garlic powder

1/4 t. salt
5 T. butter, melted
2 16-oz. loaves frozen bread
   dough, thawed
1/2 c. grated Parmesan cheese

Whisk together eggs, onions, parsley, garlic powder, salt and butter until well blended. Pinch off walnut-size pieces of dough and roll into balls. Dip into egg mixture and arrange to cover the bottom of a greased Bundt® pan. Sprinkle lightly with cheese. Repeat, layering to fill pan. Set aside, loosely covered, and let rise until double in size. Bake at 350 degrees for 30 minutes, or until golden. Makes 10 servings.

If you can't make the farmers' market early in the day, stop by near closing time. Some vendors will sell veggies at a discount to avoid packing the day's leftovers to take home.

Asparagus Bread

Tina Willingham
Grawn, MI

This recipe was given to me by my mother. No matter where it's served, there's never enough to go around. I always make several loaves at a time, and in fact, it's an easy way to get my children to eat asparagus!

3 eggs, beaten	3 c. all-purpose flour
1 c. oil	1/4 t. baking powder
1-2/3 c. sugar	1 t. baking soda
1 c. brown sugar, packed	1 t. salt
2 t. vanilla extract	1 T. cinnamon
3/4 lb. asparagus, grated	Optional: 1/2 c. chopped nuts

Whisk together eggs, oil, sugar, brown sugar and vanilla. Add asparagus; mix lightly. In a separate bowl, whisk remaining ingredients except nuts, if using. Add flour mixture to liquid mixture; stir to blend. Stir in nuts, if using. Divide mixture equally between 2 lightly greased 9"x5" loaf pans. Bake at 325 degrees for one hour, or until center tests done. Makes 2 loaves.

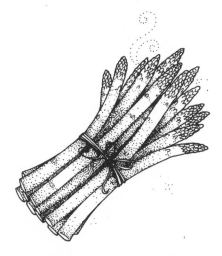

A quick asparagus side...toss trimmed spears on the grill, brush with olive oil and season with salt and pepper. Grill about 5 minutes and then enjoy!

Crockery Black Bean Soup

Beth Kramer
Port Saint Lucie, FL

*When last year's summer garden was full, I paired up fresh veggies
with pantry items in my slow cooker. This recipe was
the result and we absolutely love it!*

1 T. olive oil
2 red onions, chopped
1 red pepper, chopped
1 green pepper, chopped
4 cloves garlic, minced
4 t. ground cumin
16-oz. pkg. dried black beans
1 T. canned chopped chipotle
  chiles

7 c. hot water
2 T. lime juice
2 t. kosher salt
1/4 t. pepper
1 c. plain yogurt
1/2 c. plum tomatoes, seeded
  and chopped
Garnish: chopped fresh cilantro

Heal oil in a skillet over medium-high heat. Add onions and peppers;
sauté until tender. Stir in garlic and cumin; cook one minute. Use a
slotted spoon to transfer mixture to a slow cooker. Add beans, chiles
and hot water. Cover and cook on high setting for 6 hours. Transfer
2 cups bean mixture to a blender; purée until smooth. Return mixture
to slow cooker; stir in remaining ingredients except garnish. Garnish
servings with cilantro. Serves 6.

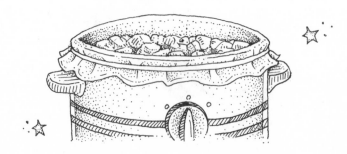

*Slow-cooker liner bags make clean-up super easy...
more time for fun with family & friends!*

Eva's Fruit Cobbler

Shelley Turner
Boise, ID

Gramma Eva was absolutely the best cook. She lived in a little town reminiscent of Mayberry where her homecooked meals were famous. Tried & true, this dessert recipe has been around for generations.

4 c. rhubarb, sliced
4 c. strawberries, hulled and
   halved
1 c. sugar, divided
1/4 c. water
2 T. apple juice
1 T. cornstarch
1 c. all-purpose flour

1 t. baking powder
1/4 t. baking soda
1/4 t. salt
1/4 c. butter
1/2 c. buttermilk
1/2 t. almond extract
Garnish: coarse sugar

In a large skillet, combine fruit, 3/4 cup sugar and water; bring to a boil. Reduce heat, cover and simmer for 10 minutes. Combine apple juice and cornstarch in a container with a tight-fitting lid; shake well to blend. Stir into fruit and cook until mixture thickens. Transfer mixture to a lightly greased 2-quart casserole dish. Set aside. Combine remaining dry ingredients, including remaining sugar, in a bowl. Cut in butter with a pastry blender or 2 forks until mixture resembles crumbs. Stir together buttermilk and extract; add to dough. Stir to blend well and drop by tablespoonfuls onto hot fruit. Sprinkle with coarse sugar. Bake at 400 degrees for 20 minutes, or until golden. Makes 8 servings.

If you pick up a rhubarb starter plant this spring, keep in mind it probably won't be big enough to harvest this year. However, next spring, you can cut stalks as soon as they grow to about the size of your finger. Remember only the stalks are edible...the leaves should be tossed into the compost bin!

Apple Blush Pie

Katherine Barrett
Bellevue, WA

This recipe goes back about 80 years in my family. It was always made from the apples from the trees in our yard.

5 apples, cored, peeled and
    sliced
3/4 c. sugar
15-1/4 oz. can crushed
    pineapple

1/3 c. red cinnamon candies
2 T. instant tapioca, uncooked
3 T. butter, softened
2 9-inch pie crusts

Combine all ingredients together except crusts. Place one crust in a 9" pie plate; top with apple mixture. Cut remaining crust into 1/2-inch strips; form a lattice pattern over filling. Bake at 425 degrees for 10 minutes, then reduce temperature to 350 degrees and bake an additional 30 minutes. Serves 8.

Making a lattice-top crust is easy as pie! Begin by arranging half the pastry strips lengthwise. Gently bend back every other strip and lay a new strip over it crosswise. Straighten the bent strips and soon the over-under basket weave will begin to show. Simply repeat with the remaining dough, trim the edges, crimp to seal and bake.

Fabulous Zucchini Brownies

Brenda Ervin
Festus, MO

When the zucchini start coming in, I am always looking for ways to use them. This recipe was given to me by a friend, and when I took it to our family reunion no one could believe that zucchini could be so good!

1-1/2 c. sugar
1/2 c. oil
2 t. vanilla extract
2 c. all-purpose flour
1/2 c. baking cocoa

1 t. baking soda
1 t. salt
2 c. zucchini, shredded
1/2 c. chopped pecans

Mix sugar, oil and vanilla; set aside. In a separate bowl, whisk together flour, cocoa, baking soda and salt. Blend in sugar mixture, zucchini and nuts. Pour into a lightly oiled 13"x9" baking pan and bake at 350 degrees for 25 to 30 minutes. Cut into squares. Makes about 1-1/2 dozen.

Dessert recipes including zucchini are a great way to use up that surplus that inevitably comes in mid-summer if you have a garden. Try new recipes for sweet breads, cakes, brownies and cookies...all are yummy!

Peanut Butter-Oat Bars

Jennifer Martineau
Gooseberry Patch

For brownie-like bars, bake closer to 20 minutes,
if you'd like them a bit crunchier, bake for 25 minutes.

1/2 c. whole-wheat flour
1 t. cinnamon
1/2 t. baking soda
1/8 t. sea salt
3/4 c. crunchy peanut butter
1/4 c. brown sugar, packed
1/3 c. honey
1 egg
2 egg whites

2 T. sunflower or olive oil
2 t. vanilla extract
2 c. long-cooking oats,
  uncooked
1 c. sweetened dried cranberries
  or raisins
1/2 c. sliced almonds
1/2 c. white or dark chocolate
  chips

Whisk together flour, cinnamon, baking soda and salt in a small bowl. In a separate bowl, beat peanut butter, brown sugar and honey with an electric mixer on medium speed. Beat egg and whites in a separate bowl; add to peanut butter mixture. Mix in oil and vanilla. Add flour mixture; stir in remaining ingredients. Spread into a greased 13"x9" baking pan, using the back of a spatula to spread easily. Bake at 350 degrees for 20 to 25 minutes. Cut into squares. Makes about 15 to 18 bars.

Shop flea-market sales for vintage-y doll houses. They're oh-so cute holding guest towels in the bathroom or tea towels in the kitchen. You can even use them to corral mail and desk supplies!

Berry Patch Bread

Jill Burton
Gooseberry Patch

Try topping slices with a drizzle of honey or
spread with strawberry cream cheese.

1-1/2 c. all-purpose flour
1/2 t. baking soda
1/2 t. salt
1/2 t. nutmeg
1/2 t. cinnamon
1 c. sugar

1/3 c. powdered sugar
2 eggs, beaten
2/3 c. oil
1-1/2 c. raspberries
1 c. chopped black walnuts

Stir together dry ingredients; set aside. Whisk eggs and oil together;
fold in berries. Add to flour mixture; stir in nuts. Pour mixture into a
greased and floured 9"x5" loaf pan. Bake at 350 degrees for one hour,
or until center tests done. Makes one loaf.

When adding chocolate chips, berries or nuts to cake and
bread batters, sometimes they sink to the bottom of the pan.
You can remedy this by tossing them in about 1/4 cup
of flour before adding to the batter.

Blueberry-Orange Muffins

Mary Hubbard
Fortine, MT

I love to make muffins for my family & friends. I make various kinds,
but this recipe is one of my favorites. We enjoy them with a tall
glass of milk, or served in a bowl, split and topped with milk.

1 c. quick-cooking oats,
   uncooked
1-1/4 c. plus 4 t. orange juice,
   divided
2 t. orange zest
1 c. oil
3 eggs, beaten

3 c. all-purpose flour
1 c. sugar
4 t. baking powder
1 t. salt
1/2 t. baking soda
3 c. blueberries
1/2 c. powdered sugar

Mix oats, 1-1/4 cups juice and zest; blend in oil and eggs. Set aside.
Stir together remaining ingredients except berries and powdered sugar.
Add oat mixture; blend lightly. Fold in blueberries. Spoon batter into
greased muffin cups, filling 2/3 full. Bake at 375 degrees for 15 to
18 minutes. Combine powdered sugar and remaining orange juice;
drizzle over cooled muffins. Makes about one dozen.

A little time and some trimmings can create a very fun
cookbook journal! Top the cover of a sweet little vintage-y
composition notebook with copies of handwritten recipe
cards and colorful retro kitchen labels, a bit of rick rack
trim and you're done. Now, it's ready to fill with
favorite recipes, memories and photos.

Soft Pumpkin Cookies

Kimberly Stine
Milford, PA

One of my children's favorite fall cookies.

2-1/2 c. all-purpose flour
1 t. baking powder
1 t. baking soda
1-1/2 t. cinnamon
1/2 t. salt

1-1/2 c. sugar
1/2 c. butter, softened
1 c. canned pumpkin
1 egg, beaten
1 t. vanilla extract

Combine flour, baking powder, baking soda, cinnamon and salt in a bowl. Beat together sugar and butter in a separate bowl until blended. Stir pumpkin, egg and vanilla until smooth. Gradually add flour and sugar mixtures and stir well. Drop by rounded tablespoonfuls onto greased baking sheets. Bake at 350 degrees for 15 to 18 minutes, or until edges are firm. Cool on baking sheets for 2 minutes, then transfer to a wire rack. Cool completely; drizzle glaze over cookies. Makes about 2 dozen.

Glaze:

2 c. powdered sugar
3 T. milk

1 T. butter, melted
1 t. vanilla extract

Combine ingredients in a small bowl; mix until smooth.

I had rather be on my farm
than be emperor of the world.
- George Washington

Strawberry-Rhubarb Pie

Shar Toliver
Boeblingen, Germany

Our family relocated to North Carolina last year where strawberries are plentiful. I decided to make a pie using the best of what is grown locally and this is the result. The combination of a sweet crust with a tart filling is the perfect taste of summer.

5 c. strawberries, hulled and chopped
2 stalks rhubarb, peeled and diced
3/4 c. brown sugar, packed
1/2 c. sugar
1/4 c. all-purpose flour
2 T. cornstarch
1/8 t. salt
1/2 t. cinnamon
9-inch pie crust
1-1/2 T. butter, diced

Combine strawberries and rhubarb; set aside. Sift together sugars, flour, cornstarch, salt and cinnamon. Stir into strawberry mixture. Place crust in a 9" pie plate; chill for 10 minutes. Spoon strawberry mixture into crust; dot with butter. Sprinkle Crumb Topping over filling. Bake at 400 degrees for 50 to 60 minutes, or until topping is golden. Set pie on a wire rack to cool for 2 hours. Makes 8 servings.

Crumb Topping:

3 T. all-purpose flour
1 T. sugar
1/8 t. salt
1 T. butter, softened

Mix together flour, sugar and salt; cut in butter until crumbly.

Bake mini pies to
share with friends...
they'll be delighted!

Just Peachy Blueberry Crisp

Kristin Pittis
Dennison, OH

*I came up with this recipe when I had a basket
of fresh peaches...it's so good!*

3 c. peaches, pitted, peeled and
  sliced
1/2 c. blueberries
2 t. cinnamon-sugar
1 c. all-purpose flour

1 c. brown sugar, packed
1/2 c. butter
3/4 c. long-cooking oats,
  uncooked

Arrange peaches and blueberries in a buttered 8"x8" baking pan.
Sprinkle with cinnamon-sugar; toss gently to coat. Combine flour and
brown sugar; cut in butter and oats. Sprinkle mixture evenly over
peaches. Bake at 350 degrees for 40 to 45 minutes. Serves 6 to 8.

*To keep berries at their sweetest and juiciest, set an ice-filled
cooler in the car and tuck baskets of berries inside for
the ride home. Keep them refrigerated and use in a
favorite recipe within a couple of days.*

Mom's Blackberry Cake

Rachel Pence
Hope, IN

*My mom makes this yummy cake each year for my birthday. This can
also be baked in a 13"x9" baking pan...simply bake for 40 minutes.*

18-1/2 oz. pkg. white cake mix
   with pudding
3-oz. pkg. red raspberry gelatin
   mix
1 c. oil

1/2 c. milk
4 eggs
1 c. blackberries
1 c. sweetened flaked coconut
1 c. chopped pecans

Combine dry cake and pudding mixes with oil and milk; mix well.
Add eggs, one at a time, beating well after each addition. Fold in
blackberries, coconut and pecans. Pour into 3 greased 9" round cake
pans. Bake at 350 degrees for 25 to 30 minutes. Cool for 10 minutes
before removing to wire racks to cool completely. Spread tops of layers
with frosting and assemble cake. Spread remaining frosting over sides.
Serves 10 to 12.

Frosting:

1/2 c. butter, softened
16-oz. pkg. powdered sugar
4 to 5 T. milk

1/2 c. blackberries, crushed
1/2 c. sweetened flaked coconut
1/2 c. chopped pecans

Beat together butter and powdered sugar. Add milk and berries; beat
for 2 minutes. Stir in coconut and pecans.

Oatmeal-Carrot Cookies

Diana Carlile
Chatham, IL

My daughter, Andrea, loves these moist cookies.
They're one of her favorites!

3/4 c. margarine
3/4 c. brown sugar, packed
1/2 c. sugar
1-3/4 c. all-purpose flour,
   divided
1 egg, beaten
1 t. baking powder
1/4 t. baking soda

1/2 t. cinnamon
1 t. vanilla extract
2 c. quick-cooking oats,
   uncooked
1 c. carrots, peeled and
   shredded
Optional: 1/2 c. raisins

Blend margarine until soft. Add sugars and 1/2 cup flour; mix well.
Add remaining ingredients except oats, carrots and raisins. Beat well.
Add remaining flour; mix well. Stir in oats, carrots and raisins, if
using. Drop by rounded teaspoonfuls onto ungreased baking sheets.
Bake at 375 degrees for 10 minutes. Makes 3 dozen.

Mix & match mugs can be found at thrift shops in a variety
of sizes and colors. Set one at each place setting to
hold a yummy sampling of homemade cookies.

Gram's Zucchini Cookies

Sharon Levandowski
Hoosick Falls, NY

For the best results, be sure to beat batter again
if it sits for more than 2 to 3 minutes.

3/4 c. butter, softened
1-1/2 c. sugar
1 egg, beaten
1 t. vanilla extract
1-1/2 c. zucchini, grated
2-1/2 c. all-purpose flour
2 t. baking powder

1 t. cinnamon
1/2 t. salt
1 c. chopped walnuts or
   almonds
6-oz. pkg. semi-sweet chocolate
   chips

Blend together butter and sugar in a bowl; beat in egg and vanilla. Stir in zucchini. In a separate bowl, combine flour, baking powder, cinnamon and salt; gradually add to butter mixture. Stir in nuts and chocolate chips. Drop by heaping teaspoonfuls onto greased baking sheets. Bake at 350 degrees for 13 to 15 minutes, or until golden. Remove to wire racks to cool. Makes 4 dozen.

Dessert in a dash...spoon ice cream into serving dishes,
top with fresh berries, toasted almonds and a drizzle
of honey. Garnish with mint leaves...yum!

Sugar-Free Cherry Pie

Barbara Schmeckpeper
Minooka, IL

With so many fresh cherries in the grocery stores and farmers' markets, I just had to buy a bunch and make a cherry pie. Recipes usually call for tart red cherries and then I need to add sugar. In my hometown, I find Bing and Rainier cherries...so I tried using half of each with no sugar in the filling. I just finished making it and it turned out so well, I had to send you the recipe!

5 c. Bing or Rainier cherries,
   pitted and halved
2 T. lemon juice
2-1/2 t. cornstarch

1/2 t. salt
1 T. butter, diced
Garnish: milk
Optional: sugar

Stir together cherries, lemon juice, cornstarch and salt; set aside. Arrange one portion of Homemade Pie Crust dough in a 9" pie plate. Spoon in cherry mixture; dot with butter. Cover with remaining dough. Flute edges and vent top. Bake at 425 degrees for 30 minutes. Brush top with milk; sprinkle with sugar, if desired. Bake for an additional 10 minutes. Serves 6 to 8.

Homemade Pie Crust:

1-3/4 c. all-purpose flour
1 t. salt

1/2 c. oil
1/4 c. cold water

Mix together flour and salt. Add oil; mix with a fork. Add water, one tablespoon at a time, mixing gently with a fork after each addition. Divide dough in half, pat into balls and flatten slightly. Roll out one portion of dough on a lightly floured surface. Roll dough to 1/4-inch thickness. Repeat with remaining dough.

Peach Flip-Overs

Melissa Luck
West Plains, MO

I had so many peaches from the farmers' market, that I popped the extras in the freezer. Try them with peach ice cream...perfect for this recipe!

2 to 3 peaches, pitted, peeled
  and sliced
2 t. butter
1/4 t. nutmeg
1 t. cinnamon
2 to 3 T. pumpkin pie spice
1 t. brown sugar, packed

1/4 c. sugar
1 to 2 t. vanilla extract
8-oz. tube refrigerated crescent
  rolls
ground ginger to taste
Garnish: powdered sugar,
  cinnamon

Add peaches, butter, spices, sugars and vanilla to a saucepan over medium heat. Simmer for 10 minutes; reduce heat to low. Separate and arrange crescent roll dough on a lightly greased baking sheet; sprinkle with ginger. Bake at 375 degrees for 5 minutes. Remove from oven and top each with one tablespoon peach mixture. Roll into a crescent; secure with a toothpick. Return to the oven for 5 to 10 minutes, or until golden. Sprinkle with powdered sugar and cinnamon. Makes 8 servings.

Fresh Peach Ice Cream

Jennifer Smith
Hebron, OH

This is delicious topped with toasted walnuts or slivered almonds.

4 peaches, pitted, peeled and
  chopped
14-oz. can sweetened
  condensed milk

juice of 1 lemon
1-1/4 c. whipping cream

Combine all ingredients except whipping cream in a food processor. Process until smooth; strain and set aside. Beat cream until stiff peaks form; fold into peach mixture. Place into an ice cream maker; freeze according to manufacturer's directions. Makes 1/2 gallon.

Generations Rhubarb Bread

Kathie Poritz
Burlington, WI

I've had this recipe for years, and my daughters still request this bread every rhubarb season. Now, I have my grandchildren helping me harvest rhubarb which I actually planted just for this recipe!

1-1/2 c. rhubarb, finely diced
1 c. brown sugar, packed
1 c. sugar
1 c. milk
1 t. vinegar
2-1/2 c. all-purpose flour

2/3 c. oil
1 egg, beaten
1 t. baking soda
1 t. salt
1 t. vanilla extract
Optional: 1/2 c. chopped nuts

Sprinkle rhubarb with sugars; set aside. Stir together milk and vinegar. Add remaining ingredients except nuts; stir until thoroughly blended. Stir in rhubarb mixture and nuts, if using. Mix well and pour into 2 greased and floured 9"x5" loaf pans. Sprinkle with topping. Bake at 350 degrees for 50 to 60 minutes, until toothpick tests clean. Makes 2 loaves.

Topping:

1/2 c. sugar
1 t. cinnamon

1 T. butter

Mix ingredients with a fork until crumbly.

Don't forget to visit U-Pick farms and roadside stands that dot the country roads in the summertime. They'll have loads of fruits, veggies and flowers for you to take home and enjoy.

Sweet Strawberry Bread

Caroline Schiller
Bayport, NY

*I taught for 41 years, and every Friday one of our faculty members
served breakfast. When it was my turn, I loved to bake breads...
this was one recipe everyone enjoyed.*

3 c. all-purpose flour
1 t. baking soda
1 t. salt
1-1/2 t. cinnamon
2 c. sugar

4 eggs
1-1/2 c. oil
2 c. strawberries, hulled and
 sliced
1-1/4 c. chopped walnuts

In a large bowl, combine flour, baking soda, salt, cinnamon and sugar.
Add eggs, one at a time, beating well after each addition. Stir in oil;
add remaining ingredients. Divide batter between 2 greased and
floured 9"x5" loaf pans. Bake at 350 degrees for one hour. Makes
2 loaves.

*The easiest fruit dip ever...combine a 7-ounce jar of
marshmallow creme with a 12-ounce container
of softened cream cheese. It's that simple!*

Green Tomato Pie

Abigail Bunce
Drain, OR

*This pie is one of my grandfather's favorites. In fact, it tastes
so much like apples, that I really like it too!*

4 c. green tomatoes, peeled and
   sliced
1 T. lemon juice
3 T. all-purpose flour

1-1/2 c. sugar
1 t. cinnamon
2 9-inch pie crusts

Set aside tomatoes in a colander to drain; toss with lemon juice.
Whisk flour, sugar and cinnamon together; sprinkle over tomatoes
and toss to coat. Place one crust in a 9" pie plate; spoon in filling. Top
with remaining crust; flute edges and vent as desired. Bake at
450 degrees for 15 minutes, reduce oven temperature to 350 degrees
and bake an additional 45 to 60 minutes. Makes 6 to 8 servings.

*If you still have lots of green tomatoes and the first frost
is on its way, bring them inside to ripen. Arrange the
tomatoes inside a cardboard box lined with shredded paper.
Top the tomatoes with a layer of newspaper and in
about 3 to 4 weeks they'll be rosy red.*

Old-Fashioned Cream Pie

Janie Reed
Gooseberry Patch

My grandma, like most grandmas, was an excellent cook. There was only one recipe she made that I couldn't reproduce when I started my own home. Since Grandma didn't have recipes written down, I spent an afternoon with her, watching her make the pies and enjoying them fresh from the oven. What a wonderful day we had! Years later, when Grandma was no longer with us, I brought this pie to a reunion and it was a huge hit.

1 c. brown sugar, packed	1/4 t. salt
1/2 c. sugar	1-1/4 c. evaporated milk
1 T. all-purpose flour	1 t. vanilla extract
2 eggs, beaten	9-inch pie crust
1 T. butter	

Combine all ingredients except crust; set aside. Place crust in a 9" pie plate; flute edges to form a rim. Pour in filling. Bake at 375 degrees about 45 minutes, or until filling rises, then just starts to fall. Cool slightly before slicing. Makes 6 to 8 servings.

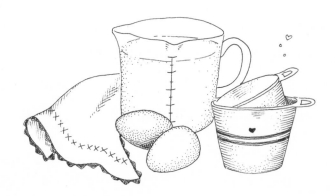

Even when you're on vacation, ask around and find a farmers' market nearby. It's great to taste locally grown foods that might not be available in your hometown.

Grandma Rose's Carrot Cake

Marge Schick
Portage, IN

My grandmother came here in 1912 from Austria. My sisters can remember her making strudel with paper-thin dough and apple filling. While I don't remember that, I do remember her carrot cake. It was the best ever...none today even compare!

2 c. sugar	4 t. baking powder
1/4 c. oil	1 t. baking soda
4 eggs	2 t. cinnamon
1 t. vanilla extract	2 c. carrots, peeled and grated
3 c. all-purpose flour	1 c. chopped walnuts
1 t. salt	

Beat sugar and oil together. Add eggs, one at a time, beating well after each addition. Stir in vanilla; set aside. Sift together dry ingredients until well blended; add to sugar mixture. Fold in carrots and nuts. Pour into a lightly greased and floured tube cake pan. Bake at 350 degrees for one hour, or until a toothpick inserted near the center comes out clean. Set aside to cool. Spread Cream Cheese Frosting over cake. Serves 12.

Cream Cheese Frosting:

8-oz. pkg. cream cheese, softened	1 t. vanilla extract
	1/8 t. salt
1 t. milk	16-oz. pkg. powdered sugar

Beat cream cheese until smooth; add milk, vanilla and salt. Gradually beat in powdered sugar until smooth.

Check thrift stores or barn sales for old-fashioned cake baskets or tin cake carriers. Both are the perfect shape and size for toting a cake to reunions, picnics or potlucks.

Grandma's Zucchini Bread

Stefanie Schmidt
Las Vegas, NV

Growing up, my favorite harvest memory was getting the chance to go over to my grandma's house. She would let me go out into the yard and pick the zucchini. We'd then use the best ones to make this bread. She would let me set out the ingredients and do the mixing, and afterward, we'd talk and enjoy slices of her delicious zucchini bread.

3 c. all-purpose flour
1 t. salt
1/4 t. baking powder
1 t. baking soda
1 T. ground cinnamon
3 eggs, beaten

1 c. oil
2 t. vanilla extract
2-1/4 c. sugar
2 zucchini, shredded
1/2 c. chopped walnuts

Sift flour, salt, baking powder, baking soda and cinnamon together; set aside. Beat eggs, oil, vanilla and sugar together; add to flour mixture and blend well. Stir in zucchini and nuts until well combined. Pour batter into 2 lightly oiled 8"x4" loaf pans. Bake at 325 degrees for 40 to 60 minutes. Cool in pans on a wire rack for 20 minutes. Remove from pans and let cool. Makes 2 loaves.

Stir 2 tablespoons of honey into one cup of softened butter...delicious on quick breads.

Mulberry Buckle

Mary Murray
Gooseberry Patch

Come July, we pick mulberries from the tree in our backyard, then whip up this yummy dessert...perfect for Pioneer Day or a family night treat. It's equally good with fresh raspberries or blackberries.

2 c. all-purpose flour
2-1/2 t. baking powder
1/4 t. salt
1/2 c. shortening

3/4 c. sugar
1 egg, beaten
1/2 c. milk
2 c. mulberries

Stir together flour, baking powder and salt; set aside. Blend shortening and sugar until light and fluffy. Add egg and beat well. Add flour mixture and milk alternately to egg mixture, beating until smooth. Pour into a greased 9"x9" baking pan; top with mulberries and Crumb Topping. Bake at 350 degrees for 50 to 60 minutes, or until golden. Serve warm. Makes 9 servings.

Crumb Topping:

1/2 c. all-purpose flour
1/2 c. sugar

1/2 t. cinnamon
1/4 c. butter

Sift together flour, sugar and cinnamon. Cut in butter until mixture resembles coarse crumbs.

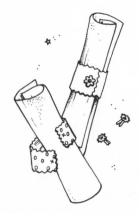

Cute napkin cuffs...in minutes. Use pinking shears to cut out a rectangle of fabric and wrap it around a napkin. Keep the ends in place with a perky flower brad, easily found in craft stores. Simply cut and "x" in the rectangle fabric and put the brad through the hole.

Rhubarb Upside-Down Cake

Donna Tennant
Jasper, IN

My grandmother used to grow rhubarb, and as a child I used to wonder why anyone would want to eat such a thing. Of course being a child and breaking off a piece and chewing on it would have given anyone that thought! But try it in this cake, and I promise you will flip for rhubarb!

3 c. rhubarb, diced
1-1/2 c. sugar
6-oz. pkg. strawberry gelatin
   mix

2 c. mini marshmallows
18-1/2 oz. pkg. yellow or white
   cake mix

Combine rhubarb, sugar and gelatin mix. Pour into a lightly greased 13"x9" baking pan. Sprinkle with marshmallows; set aside. Prepare cake batter according to package directions; pour over marshmallows. Bake at 350 degrees for 45 minutes. Let cool, then invert onto a cake plate to serve. Serves 12.

Try grilling summertime fruit for a new dessert idea.
Brush fruit slices lightly with melted butter and grill
over medium heat until golden. Add a sprinkling of
cinnamon or brown sugar for a little sweetness.

Apple Crumble

Wendy Lee Paffenroth
Pine Island, NY

This recipe uses a cake mix making it super-simple!

1/2 c. butter, softened
18-1/2 oz. pkg. yellow cake mix
1/2 c. sweetened flaked coconut
3 c. apples, cored, peeled and
    thinly sliced
1/2 c. sugar

1 t. cinnamon
1 egg, beaten
1-1/2 t. vanilla extract
1 c. sour cream
Garnish: whipped cream

Combine butter and cake mix in a bowl. Use a pastry cutter or two knives to blend mixture until it resembles coarse crumbs; stir in coconut. Pat mixture into the bottom of an ungreased 13"x9" baking pan. Bake at 350 degrees for 8 to 10 minutes or until golden. Arrange apple slices in rows over warm crust. Stir together sugar and cinnamon; sprinkle over apple slices. Blend egg and extract into sour cream; drizzle over apples. Return to oven and bake for an additional 25 minutes or until apples are tender. Serve warm with dollops of whipped cream. Makes 6 to 8 servings.

It's easy to keep your just-picked apples fresh for the winter. Unfold a sheet of newspaper and tear it into quarters. Set an apple on a square of newspaper and fold it up and around the apple. Give the corners a slight twist to keep the apple wrapped. Arrange wrapped apples in a cardboard box stored in an unheated basement or attic and they'll stay fresh for 3 or 4 months.

A handy Conversion Chart
for our favorite fruits & veggies!

Apples	1 lb. = 2-3/4 cups, diced or sliced
Beets	1 lb. = 2 cups, sliced
Bell Peppers	1 large = 1 cup, diced
Berries	1 lb. = 2 cups
Broccoli	1 lb. = 4-1/2 cups
Cabbage	1 lb. = 4 cups, shredded
Carrots	1 lb. = 4 cups, sliced, 3 cups, shredded and 2-1/2 cups, diced
Cauliflower	1 lb. = 1-1/2 cups
Cauliflower	16-oz. bag frozen = 4 cups fresh
Celery	1 large stalk = 3/4 cup, diced
Cherries	15-oz. can = 1-3/4 to 2 cups fresh
Corn	10-oz. pkg. frozen = 2 cups fresh
Garlic	3 large cloves = 1 tablespoon, minced
Green Beans	1 lb. = 3 cups
Green Beans	9-oz. pkg. frozen = 1-2/3 cups fresh
Green Beans	1 lb. fresh = 3 cups
Green Onions	4 = 1 cup, sliced
Herbs	1 teaspoon dried = 3 teaspoons fresh
Onions	1 lb. = 2-1/2 cups, chopped
Parsley	1 bunch = 1-1/3 to 1-1/2 cups, chopped
Pears	1 medium = 1/2 cup, sliced
Peas	1 lb. = 1-1/4 cups, shelled
Peas	10-oz. pkg. frozen = 2 cups fresh
Potatoes	1 lb. = 2-1/4 cups, cooked; 1-3/4 cups, mashed
Pumpkin	15-oz. can = 2 cups
Spinach	12-oz. bag = 5 cups; 1-3/4 cups cooked
Spinach	10-oz. pkg. frozen, chopped = 1-1/8 cups fresh
Squash	1 lb. = 1 cup, mashed
Tomatoes	28-oz. can, whole = 1-1/3 cups, chopped
Tomatoes	1 lb. = 3 cups, chopped
Zucchini	1 lb. = 3 cups, sliced

INDEX

INDEX

Send us your favorite recipe!

*and the memory that makes it special for you!** If we select your recipe for a brand-new **Gooseberry Patch** cookbook, your name will appear right along with it... and you'll receive a FREE copy of the book!

Submit your recipe on our website at
www.gooseberrypatch.com

Or mail to:

Gooseberry Patch · Attn: Cookbook Dept.
P.O. Box 190 · Delaware, OH 43015

*Please include the number of servings and all other necessary information!

Since 1992, we've been publishing country cookbooks for every kitchen and for every meal of the day! Each has hundreds of budget-friendly recipes, using ingredients you already have on hand. Their lay-flat binding makes them easy to use and each is filled with hand-drawn artwork and plenty of personality.

Have a taste for more?

Call us toll-free at
1·800·854·6673

Find us here too!

Get the inside scoop when you watch our product videos, read our blog and follow us on Facebook & Twitter!

www.gooseberrypatch.com

PRODUCT VIDEOS

Our NEW Blog

Find us on Facebook

Follow us on twitter

calico aprons

jams & jellies

farmgirl fare

juicy berries

sunny sweet corn

fresh Tomato

farm-fresh flowers

homebaked pies

bushel baskets

U.S. to Canadian recipe equivalents

Volume Measurements

1/4 teaspoon	1 mL
1/2 teaspoon	2 mL
1 teaspoon	5 mL
1 tablespoon = 3 teaspoons	15 mL
2 tablespoons = 1 fluid ounce	30 mL
1/4 cup	60 mL
1/3 cup	75 mL
1/2 cup = 4 fluid ounces	125 mL
1 cup = 8 fluid ounces	250 mL
2 cups = 1 pint =16 fluid ounces	500 mL
4 cups = 1 quart	1 L

Weights

1 ounce	30 g
4 ounces	120 g
8 ounces	225 g
16 ounces = 1 pound	450 g

Oven Temperatures

300° F	150° C
325° F	160° C
350° F	180° C
375° F	190° C
400° F	200° C
450° F	230° C

Baking Pan Sizes

Square
8x8x2 inches	2 L = 20x20x5 cm
9x9x2 inches	2.5 L = 23x23x5 cm

Rectangular
13x9x2 inches	3.5 L = 33x23x5 cm

Loaf
9x5x3 inches	2 L = 23x13x7 cm

Round
8x1-1/2 inches	1.2 L = 20x4 cm
9x1-1/2 inches	1.5 L = 23x4 cm